What they say about this tremendously successful System:

*"The real strength in this **Make More Money Now** System is that it is EASY to use and very powerful. Right after Alvin's program, I used this System to convert a hard to handle business negotiation into a $2,000,000 sale with a commission for me of $60,000."*

—Adrian Roscow, President, Independent Telecom Ltd

"This treasure book is like Aladdin's cave. Overflowing with tremendous sparkling secrets to help you quickly move ahead in your life and your business. (Warning: Do not loan this book to anyone. You will never get it back!)"

—Dottie Walters, President, Walters International Speakers Bureau, Publisher/Editor, SHARING IDEAS Newsmagazine

*"Your powerful **Make More Money Now** concepts have led various sales teams to increased sales by improving, immediately after your seminar, the conversion rate 'contacts/contracts.'"*

—Walter Winniger, President, Wall Street Institute SA

"New material consistently well presented. I set a clear goal coming here and leave with tools to achieve it."

—Colin Hudson, Director, IMM

"… the most important learning experience in our lives."

—Erik Melander, President, Karlesholme Investments

"Alvin is the most professional and charismatic speaker I have seen in a business career that spans 25 years in marketing and selling across 11 countries."

—John McInerney, Irish Management Institute

"Excellent principles well presented."

—Leon Dicks, Head of Procurement, Sasol

"Excellent presentation to demonstrate the decision making process. Outcome always defined."

—Alfred Malle, Financial Manager, Otis Elevator

"This is a well prepared program….Alvin is an excellent trainer."

—Paul Lukas, Director, Bank Bali

"Overall presentation excellent. The course content was very much higher than similar seminars."

—Johnathan Austin, Managing Director, JH Austin Group

————◆◆◆◆◆◆————

"Very good and competent presentation, time table, contents, exercises."

—Dr Gunter Gutsman, Director, Landis & Gyr

————◆◆◆◆◆◆————

"Compact body of presentation without theoretical fluff."

—Martin Bergler, Director, Mazda

————◆◆◆◆◆◆————

"Useful and the trainer is excellent."   —Peter Volster, Premium Brokers

————◆◆◆◆◆◆————

"Very interesting and focused workshop."   —Adam Dewi, Merchandising Manager, Avon

————◆◆◆◆◆◆————

"Clear and concentrated with good direction."

—Paul Wijittongruang, Schneider Equipment

————◆◆◆◆◆◆————

"Program: very useful, Trainer: excellent—world class."

—Dan Roelvert, Executive Director, National Association Housing Developers

————◆◆◆◆◆◆————

"Program very thought provoking, very good practical implementation of the methodologies of the course."

—Rod Williams, National Field Operations manager, ERA Real Estate

————◆◆◆◆◆◆————

"All aspects of the course were very informative and Alvin really motivated me to do the best I can."

—Natalie Roll, Export Manager, TRW

————◆◆◆◆◆◆————

"Very good [to] get rapport, criteria of your negotiation partner."   —Josef Kapfer, Sony

————◆◆◆◆◆◆————

"... a world class performer. It was one of the greatest learning experiences."

—Arie Mayer, Sales Director, Time Manager International

————◆◆◆◆◆◆————

"Very good criteria, convincer."

—Rudolf Hanslik-Kupsa, Group manager, Digital Equipment

Make More Money NOW

Why Alvin G. Donovan III and Meg Northcroft can show you how to boost your persuasive power, enhance your career, and *make more money NOW*:

Internationally renowned author, speaker, entrepreneur, and TV/Radio personality Alvin G. Donovan III is considered the finest persuasion, sales, and marketing skills expert in the world. His background includes over 23 years of speaking excellence. During this time he has perfected his eminently practical, surprising, and truly effective methodologies.

Alvin presents his unique know-how—acquired through lifelong dedication to discovering and replicating the key strategies of the most successful people in the world—in an easy-to-understand and entertaining manner.

Educated in psychology, specializing in the development of advanced training technologies, Alvin's early career focused on the development of persuasion, sales and marketing technologies. He then applied these technologies to achieve spectacular results in the international business arena.

Alvin has spoken for some of the world's largest and most prestigious management institutes including Management Centre Europe in Belgium (a division of American Management Association and Europe's largest management training organization), OPWZ in Vienna, ZFU in Zurich, Irish Management Institute in Dublin, IEP in Holland, APM of Bangkok and Kotler Centre for Marketing in Jakarta, all of whom are market leaders in their fields.

Meg Northcroft manages Alvin's immensely successful international business. Meg and Alvin have been partners for 15 years, developing seminars, products and books as well as sharing a successful marriage. Meg has 15 years of international business experience as well in seminar facilitation and is an award winning art director.

Audiences have been mainly senior executives from many of the world's largest companies including:

ABB	Alcatel	AT&T
Avon	Bank Central Asia	Barclays
Canon	Citibank	Digital Equipment
DSM	Dupont	ERA
Garuda	Guinness	Hawaiian Tropic
Hilton	IBM	IMM
IT&T	Johnson&Johnson	Kimberly Clark
Kraft Jacobs	Landis & Gyr	Mastercard
Mazda	Merck	Nestle
Occidental Chemical	Otis Elevator	John Robert Powers
Procter & Gamble	Prudential	Sasol
Sony	Suchard	Sumitomo
3M	TNT	UOP
Vorwerk	Wall Street Institutes	Wella
Winterthur	Xerox	

Alvin Donovan presents his program regularly on five continents and has spoken, performed, or consulted in over 100 major cities and centers of international finance and commerce including:

New York	Chicago	San Diego	London	Brussels
Zurich	Geneva	Tokyo	Dublin	Frankfurt
Vienna	Prague	Lugano	Milan	Turin
Antwerp	Durban	Johannesburg	Pretoria	Capetown
Hong Kong	Singapore	Kuala Lumpur	Jakarta	Bangkok
Sydney	Melbourne	Perth	Oslo	Stockholm
Helsinki	Copenhagen	Tampa	Orlando	

Make More Money NOW

**Dramatic New 21-Day MONEY MAKING SYSTEM
Guaranteed to Make Everything You Say and Write
Powerful, Influential, Convincing & Instantly Lucrative.**

"The real strength in this *Make More Money Now* System is that it is
EASY to use and very powerful. Right after Alvin's program, I used this
System to convert a hard to handle business negotiation into a $2,000,000
sale with a commission for me of $60,000."

—Adrian Roscow, President, Independent Telecom Ltd.

ALVIN G. DONOVAN III
with Meg Northcroft

Edited by Warren Jamison

Copyright ©1998 by Pavillion Publishing

Pavillion Publishing
4524 Curryford Rd., Suite 237
Orlando, FL 32812

ISBN 0-9657077-0-9
Library of Congress Number 97-067420

Cataloging-in-Publication Data

Donovan, Alvin G.
       Make more money now : dramatic new 21 day money making system guaranteed /
by Alvin G. Donovan III and Meg Northcroft -- 1st ed.
       p. cm.
       Includes bibliographical references and index.
       ISBN: 0-9657077-0-9

       1. Selling.   I. Northcroft, Meg. II. Title

HF5438 25.D66 1997   658.85
                                      QBI97-40821

Printed in the United States of America

We have probably learned something from every person we have met and to list them all here would double the size of this book. We dedicate this book to our parents. With their constant support, encouragement and unconditional love we realize that we have always possessed greater riches than our wildest dreams.

Powerful persuasion techniques are packed into the following pages. All of them work with incredible effectiveness in win-win situations.

———◆•✕•◆———

To speed your learning, we practice what we preach by using **hidden outcome directives** in the text. They appear in **bold italics**. When you read the text you will also discover that we use the language patterns we teach. Sometimes this results in sentences which are not always grammatical. They are powerful however and will cause you to **make more money NOW**.

TABLE OF CONTENTS:

PART II

PART III

CHAPTER 1

How to Get the Most from this Book

Our Purpose
How this Book Will Help You Make More Money NOW
Keys to Special Helps

OUR PURPOSE

Our purpose in writing this book is to give you a tool you can rapidly use as your constant mentor while you boost your income by easily learning and applying this System. To achieve the happy outcome of rapidly boosting your income, you must first clearly *define your goals.*

Then you do what's required to reach your goals by increasing your ability to persuade others and *make more money NOW.* As your persuasive powers and income increase, you'll encounter a delightful phenomenon: doubling your income does not double your workload. Quite the contrary.

For example, business people who close only ten percent of their business opportunities work harder than their associates who close twenty percent or more of their opportunities. Generally speaking—there are exceptions, of course—the effort involved in losing the deal is at least as great as the effort involved in making the deal. Obviously, the frustration of losing is vastly greater. This explains why the top performers in any organization are more relaxed and can cope with unexpected problems better than the bottom feeders. So, rather than working harder when you're making a lot more money, your life will be easier and more enjoyable.

HOW THIS BOOK WILL HELP YOU MAKE MORE MONEY NOW

NOW that we have convinced you to *make more money NOW* as quickly as you can, let's look again at how this book will help you *do it.* It will enable you to monitor and track your progress toward increased persuasion peak performance enhancement for two reasons: first, to motivate you; second, to help you discover omissions and weaknesses you need to correct as well as strengths you can rely on *even more.*

These things work naturally. We know it because they have performed beyond expectations for thousands of people in countless situations. However, it's up to you to lift these skills, techniques, and insights off the page. In other words, you have to ***do them yourself***.

When you ***use the System correctly***, you'll be implementing what you're learning in everyday situations. ***Do this*** and you will get more of what you want when you want it.

NOW, as you study your way through this book, you will of course be working or doing whatever occupies your time. Make a point of noticing on a daily basis all the many ways your ability to persuade others is increasing.

In the bustle of daily routine, it's easy to overlook how much what you're learning is helping you. That's counterproductive. Make a practice of taking a few moments ***NOW*** and then to recognize what you're accomplishing by ***using this expertise***. Doing so will pay huge dividends by spurring you to learn even more. It's useful to encourage others; it's *vital* to encourage yourself.

Hit your study program hard. Set your sights on boosting your performance—and income—to the max. Learn all these powerful techniques so well you'll begin immediately to instinctively ***use them*** in your every presentation and contact. Make ***mastering this book*** your top priority. ***Do this*** and you'll automatically ***increase your earnings*** substantially.

The format of this book is as follows. *Why, What, How, What if.* We will begin with outcome—with the end result you are working for. We will show you *why* you would want to learn about outcome. In other words, when we teach you something, we will tell you what benefits you'll gain in return for exercising your brain to **master these skills**.

Next the book will give you information to answer all the *what* questions. The *what* part will give you all the facts about what you are learning.

Then we'll do the *how* part of these skills. The *how* involves doing an exercise which will cause you to rapidly incorporate what **you are learning** into your daily life. The 21-Day Program, located in Part II, Section A provides exercises you can use in your everyday life to naturally enhance your persuasive power.

Finally, we'll focus on the *What If* part of the skill. *What if* I use this in the real world? How can I use this in my everyday life to **make more money NOW**? The foremost thought in your mind as you do this System needs to be: "How can I begin immediately to **use this information** to cause myself to rapidly **make more money NOW**? This will also be provided to you in the 21-Day Program in Part II, Section A.

This will be somewhat like your first school years. Remember when you learned the difference between a 6 and a 9? Remember when you learned the difference between a B and a D?

While you were mastering the letters of the alphabet, you probably didn't realize then that you could go on to make sentences, paragraphs and more, and be able to express yourself in many new ways. The same easy learning of *something with enormously greater application than at first appears* will happen as you go through this book. It will happen because you'll be **learning these techniques** the same way you absorbed basic knowledge in the first grade. We will teach things in small pieces along the way; at the end of this book you'll be fully prepared to put it all together.

Most books and seminars present some wonderful ideas and theories that sound like they'd be marvelous when implemented into your daily life. Generally you don't put them into practice for either or both of two basic reasons—they don't apply to your life, or no clear ways to implement them are given. Underwhelming, to say the least.

There's a "difference that makes the difference" with this System. It gives you the ability to immediately put everything you learn into practice in your daily life. No other System does this.

However, all failure to improve can't be laid at the door of the seminar speakers and book writers. You the reader have an essential part to play. You can't merely hear or read the theories. To install new behaviors so they'll easily and naturally go to work when you need them, you have to *do the exercises*. In other words, you have to take the learning process seriously; you even have to use a little effort. Otherwise, you won't be able to use these marvelous discoveries in your daily life.

When, on the other hand, you do an exercise specifically designed to *install new behaviors,* you will profit from it in your daily life. *NOW*, since you're going to be quite busy *making more money NOW* it will also be helpful to have a constant companion to tell you exactly what to do in every situation.

The *Vade Mecum* part of this book comes in here. It's a System of grading and charting to help you monitor your progress. Use it to overcome challenges, to direct your attention to any problem areas, and to keep yourself on track in general. The vade mecum also provides some examples of formats to follow in various situations you may face.

The key to success in any enhancement System is to use a grading and charting System you can refer to frequently. This applies whether you're pursuing greater physical fitness, greater marketing skills, or greater personal development in other areas. We suggest you put your charts on the wall in a place you will see them often. Seeing the progress-tracking charts on the wall creates within you the proper motivations and drives that will enable you to continually *make more money NOW.*

So we have included all the tools you need to immediately *become more successful NOW*. All you have to do is *use them*.

NOW, having said that, don't believe a word in this book! Assume that every word written here is a lie.

Why would we write such a thing? Because we want you to use what we teach you in the real world and see for yourself what actually happens.

We are going to teach you various skills. Do the opposite of what we teach and see what effect it has on your income.

Next, do exactly as we teach; and notice how rapidly you *achieve the outcome* you desire.

Everything you learn here is designed to be used in the real world; keep that concept firmly in mind and you will constantly think of ways to *implement this* and make it work for you.

In developing this System, we wanted to know the answers to two key questions: (1) does it work? (2) how does it work? We used the following list of criteria (Criteria List):

> *Does it <u>work</u> or not, and how?*
> *Is it <u>practical</u> or not, and how?*
> *Is it <u>real</u> or not, and how?*
> *Is it <u>simple</u> or not, and how?*
> *Do I get better <u>results</u> or not, and how?*

This Criteria List of ours separates effective technologies from useless ones. This is the "difference that makes the difference" in *making more money.*

NOW, this System, when you use it exactly as laid out in this book, can work for you. The way it works is to give you tools, which when properly applied, allow you to *increase your persuasion power*. Increasing your persuasion power stimulates you to generates better results. The better results you generate will cause you to *make more money NOW.*

YOUR *Make More Money NOW* CONTRACT WITH YOURSELF

Because we want you to ***get the most*** from this book, it's critical that you imagine all the ways you're going to ***use it***. You also need to understand your inner motivations to help you ***make more money NOW***. So please fill this out completely.

Please read all eight questions before you fill in the blanks.

1. As a result of using this book, ***what do you want to be able to do*** that will make this your ***most important learning experience ever?*** (Please be very specific and state in concrete terms what you will be seeing, hearing, feeling, and how you will be making sense of it all.)

    _____

    _____

    _____

    _____

2. **What is important to you about being able to be/have/do** the answer to 1 above?

    _____

    _____

    _____

    _____

3. **What is important about that?**

    _____

    _____

    _____

    _____

4. **Because?**

_____

_____

_____

_____

5. So **ultimately, what would this mean to you?**

_____

_____

_____

_____

6. As you accomplish this, **what information about yourself** will you be presenting to others?

_____

_____

_____

_____

7. **More importantly,** what **information about yourself** will you be **presenting to yourself?**

_____

_____

_____

_____

8. What is your **evidence procedure?** What will you need to see, hear, make sense of, or

feel in order to know you have achieved the result you desire?

_____

_____

_____

_____

NOW restate your above responses below as clearly and briefly as possible.

As a result of this System, I want:

_____

_____

_____

_____

I want to do this because:

4. _____

_____

_____

_____

3. _____

_____

_____

_____

2. _____

_____

_____

_____

1. _____

_____

_____

_____

I am going to do everything it takes to accomplish this outcome!

Your signature:_____Date: _____

KEYS TO SPECIAL HELPS

Personal Training Tips:

> *provide very important information you can immediately use.*
> *They are given in lightly shaded boxes like this one.*

Definitions:

> *of special terms used in this book are given in unshaded boxes like this one.*

"The best way to predict your future is to design it NOW."
—Alvin G. Donovan III

CHAPTER 2

Managing Goals: Outcome Determination, Generation, and Realization

BENEFITS OF THIS CHAPTER

Here are the benefits you'll gain by putting this chapter to work in your daily routine:

- *It will boost your ability to motivate yourself for action and avoid procrastination.*
- *You will install positive substantive generative change strategism to achieve the future you desire.*
- *You will learn the secret to cause peak performance enhancement in all areas of your life.*
- *You will learn how to design and engineer your money future.*

THE PROCEDURE FOR DETERMINING OUTCOME

Would it be helpful to have a way to always keep on track to your desired outcome in every opportunity you have? Certainly it would. All right, let's move on to making it happen. First, let's consider categories of people. Many divide people into two categories, winners and losers. Others divide people into three categories:

➡ *Those who make it happen*

➡ *Those who watch it happen*

➡ *Those who wonder, "What happened?"*

The *second* most important question is: "Which of the three do you choose to be?" The *first* question—and by far the most important—is, *"Which of the three will you work at becoming?"* Regardless of who you *wish* to be, the energy you direct toward achieving your outcomes determines which you *will* be.

No matter what your lot in life, you must always strive to improve it. Complacency pushes you behind, not ahead. There's no such thing as standing still. Throughout life, you're either growing stronger or weaker, smarter or dumber, more healthy or more sickly, richer or poorer.

So, from *NOW* on, before starting anything, before committing yourself to any challenge, before undertaking any task, always ***determine the outcome you desire before you do it.*** The reason is simple: *the more strongly and clearly you **determine the outcome** you're seeking, the more likely you are to **get it**.*

The more you think, work, see, hear, feel, and make sense of things in terms of outcome the more likely you are to ***achieve your goals***.

What you need to do is cut new grooves in your brain that lead you towards achieving the goals you want to achieve. A way that is very useful to us is to go through a certain refocusing on a daily basis. Depending on your time schedule and your desire for results, you can do this vital procedure in one to four minutes a day:

NEW OUTCOME GENERATOR—STAGE 1

- Prime the pump. Get things started by determining what you want. Then establish how you'll know when you have it.
- Set up goal posts along the way to your outcome so you know you're moving in the right direction and also to know when you have achieved your goal.

How about starting with the outcome you want to achieve from reading this book? Imagine you could wave a magic wand, what would happen, what would you achieve after reading it? For a moment, let your imagination run wild! Dare to dream up the most exciting, wonderfully fulfilling fantasy that could ever be!

Stick with physically possible things. For example, you can imagine yourself being many years younger, or flying like Superman. Such dreams may be fun and they aren't going to happen. What you need to be looking for here is the most exciting, wonderfully fulfilling fantasy that could actually come to pass.

We want to issue a word of warning. Make sure what you wish for is what you actually want, what will make you really happy. Don't be too surprised when these wishes actually come true. We want only happy surprises.

1. It's very important to state the outcome in terms of what you want to achieve instead of what you want to avoid or discard.

Many people make this mistake because they don't realize how important it is to state your desired outcome in positive rather than negative terms. Let's explore this further. Suppose you state something along these lines, "I don't want to keep making only as much money as I am making *NOW*." Of course you don't, nobody does. But using such a negative concept as an outcome statement digs a psychological pitfall. Why? Because in order for your mind to understand that statement, you first have to imagine making only as much money as you are *NOW*, and then cancel that dismal picture out.

On the other hand, when you state something like, "I want to begin immediately to easily and naturally *make more money NOW*," you create a picture of doing exactly that. In other words you visualize success instead of failure, so you can just follow along that mental track unimpeded.

As a result of using this System, what outcome do you want to achieve? Write it here with a completion date:

_____

_____

_____

2. **Before you start the generator, define and establish what sensory-based evidence will indicate you have reached a successful conclusion.**

   How would you know you could *accomplish the goal* in a specific situation or with a specific person? What would be there? What would you need to see, hear, feel, or make sense of?

   Have you done it before? Have you accomplished this goal, or done something like it before? What did it feel like? Pay particular attention to the feelings you have had as you achieved that other goal. Really get in touch with that feeling and note exactly where it is in your body and what it feels like so that you can remember it easily. **Specify that *feeling of success*. Write it here:**

   _____

   _____

   _____

   _____

NOW we're ready to begin:

NEW OUTCOME GENERATOR—STAGE 2

1. Determine the new outcome you want to generate. Ask yourself, "After I have already achieved my new goal, what will I look like? (Put your eyes and head down and to the <u>left</u>.)

2. Picture yourself achieving your goal as though you're watching yourself in a movie. (Look up and to the <u>right</u>.) **Make the picture bigger, clearer, closer, and brighter—add vivid colors and motion.** This is a movie of people in action.

3. Step into the picture so you feel yourself doing what you pictured. (Put your eyes and head down and to the <u>right</u>.)

4. Compare these feelings to feelings from a similar past success. (Keep your eyes and head turned down and to the <u>right</u>.)

5. When it feels the same, you can proceed to seize the new goal. If it does not feel the same yet, find what's missing and add it to your outcome. Then redo the process until it feels the same as the similar past success.

Why do we have you move your eyes and head in these ways? Moving your eyes and head in certain ways allows you to empower certain parts of your brain. For example, moving your head and eyes up and to the right or left can permit you to more easily make mental pictures.

Let's use the example of *making more money NOW*. Write down that you want to *make more money NOW*. Imagine what it feels like to *make more money NOW*. Really give dynamic attention to the feelings it produces. Make a note of those feelings here:

_____

_____

Use whatever words evoke the feeling of the most exciting, wonderfully fulfilling fantasy that could ever be! Next, put your eyes and head down and to the left as you ask yourself, "After I can already *make more money NOW*, what will I look like?"

Next, put your eyes and head up and to the right and watch yourself *making more money NOW*. Do this as though you were watching a movie of that scene. Make sure the movie has color, is bright enough, close enough, and big enough to have real emotional impact on you.

Next, put your eyes and head down and to the right, step into the movie, and become the actor playing the lead role. As you do this, compare that feeling to the feeling of the past success above.

How did that feel? When it does feel the same, you can proceed to seize the goal. If it did not feel the same yet, find what is missing and add it. Then redo the process.

Also, just for the fun of it, redo the process again, doing the opposite of what is written above. For example, on step 1 turn your eyes and head down and to the <u>right</u>. On the rest of the steps, put your eyes and head to the <u>left</u>. Notice which one felt better for you. Continue to use the eye and head movements which feel best to you.

Most people have no challenge to move their eyes and head in the right direction. The key is the ask the right question, make the pictures come alive in your brain, and pay attention to your feelings. This takes a bit of practice and will become natural with repetition. Practice this over and over. As you begin to *use this*, you'll discover it really works to more readily *achieve the outcomes* you're seeking.

You'll further *increase your success rate* at achieving your desired outcomes when you *use this technique* frequently. In other words, constant use enables you to *make more money NOW*, and achieve the lifestyle you desire.

Do you remember reading, "Don't believe a word we say" at the beginning? Tomorrow, before every meeting, how about doing the opposite of what we have been saying? See what results you get. Notice how it effects your ability to *make more money NOW*.

The next day, before every meeting run through the New Outcome Generator and see what results you get. Notice how it effects your ability to *make more money NOW*.

You can do this with all the skills we teach you in each chapter. With one encounter or situation, do the opposite of what we teach you in that chapter. See how easily you achieve your desired outcome. With the next encounter or situation, do exactly as we teach you and see how easily you get what you want.

Okay, we have done an exercise; you have learned something. *NOW* it's time to think how you can put this new power into practice. The crucial thing is to write down your intention to use this new knowledge: we urge you to write it in the space below.

Answer these questions: "What are some of the many ways that I can already use and *apply this* in the real world?" and "How can I begin immediately to *use this information* in the real world to cause myself to rapidly *make more money NOW*?"

Write here some of the many ways you are going to immediately use this knowledge to *make more money NOW*:

_____

_____

_____

_____

Note: Exercises for this chapter can be found in Part II, Section A.

"People like most those who are most like them."
—Meg Northcroft

CHAPTER 3

Rapport and Bonding: How to Get Anyone to Instantly Fall in Love With You

BENEFITS OF THIS CHAPTER

- *Learn how to establish rapport in 30 seconds or less with anyone.*

- *Build trust into every communication.*

- *Send subliminal messages of likeness.*

- *Improve your range of responsiveness.*

- *Achieve personal and professional flexibility.*

- *Establish deep bonds of trust-quickly.*

- *Subtly determine when you have rapport with someone.*

- *Use your senses to develop understanding of others.*

- *Establish meaningful communication.*

- *Improve your responsiveness range.*

- *Build trust into your communication.*

- *Verify the current level of rapport.*

- *Get people to focus on you.*

Calibrate:

to determine, check, and make a mental note of the changes from moment to moment that you see in the person in front of you, or hear on the other end of a phone conversation.

RAPPORT

Rapport—by which we mean the art and science of *establishing* rapport—is the way to easily and naturally eliminate perceived differences between yourself and the other person.

THE PROCESS OF RAPPORT

To start with you must realize that you cannot **not** influence others in some way through **all** of your behaviors. Let us restate this essential concept in positive terms. In some way, you are certain to influence other people through all of your behaviors. This applies both to your encounters with individuals and with groups of people. It's your task to discover the most elegant means to *use this knowledge* to continually *achieve the outcomes* you desire or, failing that, you will wind up with outcomes you don't want.

So you must *realize*:

1. *Process is more important than content.* The process of how you persuade is more important than the exact words you use.

2. *You must use all your sensory acuity*— everything you see, hear, feel, think—(i.e. Skin tone or color, lower lip or breathing changes that are occurring in the person in front of you). *Use your sensory acuity* to calibrate what's going on with the other person and *achieve your outcome.*

Cycling:

> *to go through a complete round of all the key elements of a person's strategy and/or Criteria List over and over again until the person has an overwhelming desire to do as you wish.*

In other words you simply:

- Find out how *they* normally do it.
- Find out how *they* need it to be delivered. What they want, when and how many times they want it, and so on.
- *Do it that way.*

   NOTE: Your job is to elegantly elicit the process of how they prefer to make decisions based on what is personally important to them. Then you cycle though the persons strategy (as explained in Chapter 5) and/or Criteria List (as explained in Chapter 6) continually until you achieve your outcome.

WOULD IT BE HELPFUL

- to have a way to get people to naturally like you?
- to have clients immediately bond with you?
- to be able to speak with others in such a way that your message is irresistible?

How can I easily and naturally do this?

We'll focus on building rapport through becoming as much like the other person as possible—through eliminating as much of the perceived differences between us as we possibly can. *People like most those who are most like them.*

The conscious mind is best defined by what it does. It enables you to shift your attention from one thing to another. Therefore, what you are aware of is the part of you called the conscious mind.

Your *un*conscious mind contains your long term memories. It is also in charge of your automatic behaviors, often called reflex actions.

In fact, our outcome for you in this System is for you to easily, naturally, and automatically **become more persuasive NOW**, and to do this by evaluating the way you instinctively respond in persuasion situations, and then make strategic changes in your behavior that will **enhance the process.**

Our experiences indicates that human communication springs from the following sources:

- From nonverbal language such as body posture, breathing, skin color, and movement: **55 percent.**

- From our vocal behavior, which includes tone of voice, timbre, tempo and volume: **38 percent**.

- From the content, the actual words spoken: **only 7 percent!**

So you can understand that "**competent**" persuaders spend most of their time concerned with what they say, and very little about **how** they say it. By the way, do you consider yourself competent? Do you know what they call the person who graduated last in their class at medical school? Doctor!

A competent person in a given field is someone who has the minimum requirements. Someone who is only adequate. Suppose you're going in for brain surgery. Do you want the competent person who was last in their class, or do you want the best you can find?

Maybe you would even want someone who is *world class excellent*.

When Alvin was nine years old, the principal of his school gave a lecture which dramatically changed his life. She said, "Some of you will discover that you're naturally good at some things, while some of you will be better at other things. Find out what you can be the best at, and continually strive to become the best in the world at that one thing."

That's what we have chosen to do. For us, achieving competence at what we do is to meet only the minimum level of qualifications. For you, the outcome we have in mind is that you will *become world class excellent* at what you do. Because when you are the *best in the world* at what you do then obviously your service or product will be much easier to sell.

You will believe more in your service or product and that will be communicated through your demeanor, attitude and elegance with which you persuade others to realize that your concept, policy, program, cause, product, purpose, or service is the best choice for them.

Clients and customers prefer to deal with the best service or product. Have you ever heard of anyone seeking to buy from the worst company in any industry? Of course not.

Therefore, merely competent persuaders spend their preparation and rehearsal time focused on <u>what</u> they are saying—on the <u>content</u> of the message—that is to say, on the part with only a 7 percent communication rate.

How do "**world-class excellent**" persuaders elegantly convince others? They spend most of their time concerned with <u>how</u> they say their message. They work most on the part that accounts for 93 percent of actual communication. That is how they *make more money.*

NOW, **engrave these numbers on your brain, and guide yourself accordingly:**

Communication:

7% = Content (what we say)

38% = Vocal behavior (how we say it, our tone of voice, timbre, tempo, and volume).

55% = Non verbal (our skin color, breathing, body posture and movement).

Personal Training Tip #1:

People already in rapport (people who like and trust each other) were studied using video cameras. It was discovered that these people were mirroring each others posture, inflection, breathing rate, and so on. Check this for yourself. Go into a cafe, restaurant, or bar. Observe a pair of lovers, a group of businessmen, whatever. Soon you will notice that they are mirroring each others posture.

When one is sitting forward, so is the other. When one is sitting back, so is the other person. This is an unconscious pattern that people already in rapport use to understand and relate to each other. So you are going to learn to do the behaviors associated with rapport to cause the other person to immediately have rapport with you:

Rapport on the <u>physiological</u> level:

Mirror everything the other person is doing, the more closely you mirror the more deeply you go into rapport with the other person. It will be like the other person is looking in the mirror.

Mirror completely:

- **Whole body-** the person's stance or overall position.
- **Body parts-** any consistent behavioral shrugs, gestures, head nods, or any other types of shifts in their behavior.
- **Breathing-** depth and/or speed and/or displacement. (This is the most powerful form.)
- **Voice-** tonality, tempo, volume, intensity and intonation patterns.

Personal Training Tip #2:

> *When you mirror the other person's physiology and voice, and speak at their rate of breathing, your message becomes <u>irresistible</u> because it's like their own unconscious (their own inner voice) is speaking to them.*

The rate at which you breathe causes your mind to run or fluctuate at a certain rate. So your breathing rate is the "speed" at which your mind is "running." When you're breathing at the same rate as the other person you will be on the same wave length. The first step of rapport is to meet them where they are. So when you *breathe at the same rate* they are, your mind is running at the same rate as theirs.

When you *do this well,* you will make a very intriguing discovery: the other person won't want to end the phone conversation or meeting. Instead, they'll be hanging on your every word.

Also, people understand what you're saying best when you talk at the rate at which they speak.

When you talk fast, you will be more easily understood by someone who speaks fast. When you talk slowly you will be more readily be understood by someone who speaks slowly. Someone who speaks fast will be anywhere from a bit bored to rudely impatient with a slow talker. On the other hand, a slow talker will find someone who speaks fast difficult or even impossible to understand. So, in order for you to *easily and naturally persuade* someone to do what you want, you <u>must</u> speak at the same rate they do.

To recap: the rate at which someone speaks is the rate at which they think; therefore, that is the rate at which they can best understand others. So, in order for you to easily and naturally persuade someone to do what you want, you <u>must</u> speak at the same rate they do.

Personal Training Tip #3:

The key to mirroring someone's breath is to look at them and/or listen to them. Sit facing them or at a 45 degree angle, and notice which position makes it easiest for you to observe the other person's breathing. Notice the rise and fall of their shoulders against the wall behind them. Watch their nostrils open as they inhale, and close as they exhale. When someone talks they are exhaling; when they stop talking they inhale.

So, while someone is talking, you are exhaling. When they stop to take a breath, you inhale with them.

If they are not talking, when their shoulders and/or chest rise, you inhale. When their shoulders and/or chest fall, you exhale with them. Therefore you speak to a person while they are exhaling and you stop to take a breath when they are inhaling. This will have a very profound effect on the person you are speaking to. The next step is to cause yourself to go into a state of extreme desire or excitement and the person in front of you will do the same.

NOTE: The most powerful way to make rapport with someone is to mirror their breath. Mirror the depth and/or speed and/or displacement of their breathing.

HARNESS THE POWER OF PACING AND LEADING

Pacing and Leading:

Pacing is defined as talking about or doing things that are verifiable and true in a person's ongoing sensory experience. Leading is defined as doing something other than what the other person is doing or you want them to do or believe; i.e. your outcome.

Notice how easily and naturally the following concept works with daily practice: Pace (mirror) everything with a three-beat time lag to start, and rapidly narrow the time lag to zero. Then lead to see when you are in accord with the other person. Personal Training Tip #4, coming up next, tells you how to do it:

Personal Training Tip #4:

Let's say the first mirroring-suitable action the other person does is to lean forward. Wait three beats and then mirror their action by leaning forward yourself.

After your first mirroring action, watch until you observe them do something else you can mirror. Allow two beats, and then follow their movement or action.

Wait for them to perform a third mirroring-suitable action. This time reduce the time lag to one beat.

On the one after that, do what they do as they are doing it. Next, you lead by shifting your posture and seeing if they follow you or not.

When they follow you, then they are in rapport with you and you can lead them to your outcome. If they do not follow you yet, simply go back to pacing them until you get them.

Think about the normal business meeting. The people greet each other and normally make small talk for between one and three minutes to ease tension and establish a friendly atmosphere. Then someone signals the small talk is over, and both parties shift physical posture and one person will begin the business part of the meeting.

So, you pace everything the other person does when you first meet and continue to do so through the first few minutes. Then will come a time for you to change the subject, move your posture and begin your presentation. See how easy it is for them to follow you.

When they follow you, lead them to your outcome.

If they don't follow you yet, simply go back to pacing until you get them one way or another. In the real world, all encounters have moments of pacing and leading throughout.

Therefore, one of the many tests for rapport is this: lead by doing something other than what the other person is doing. When they follow you then you have achieved rapport and *NOW* are well positioned for powerful persuasion.

If they don't follow you yet, go back to pacing.

NOTE: You are already always either pacing or leading.

You might think this is something new and strange to do on a daily basis. This is something that most humans already unconsciously do to some extent with each other. You will find that *NOW* that you are conscious of this behavior you can *use it* to your advantage to more rapidly *make more money NOW*.

SENSORY ACUITY

In order for you to *make more money NOW,* you need to concentrate on developing your sensory acuity. For example, what you see, hear, feel and think. It adds enormously to your persuasive power to be able to *immediately tune yourself* to the nonverbal signals indicating a particular mood, or a change in the other person's emotional state.

Some key signals to notice are:

- **Skin color change-** lighter or darker.
- **Skin muscle tone change-** shiny or dull.
- **Lower lip changes-** expansion (lines not visible) or contraction (lines visible).
- **Breathing changes-** location, speed, shallow or deep.

The key is to <u>take a mental snapshot</u> of those elements as the meeting starts, and then continually compare your starting snapshot to what you see in front of you *NOW*. This way you can subtly determine when what you're doing has the effect you want, and also when you need to vary your behavior.

THE THREE THINGS ALL EFFECTIVE COMMUNICATORS DO

All effective communicators (top salespeople, ministers, politicians, managers, and so on) do the same three things in order to be successful:

1. They determine the outcome they want.

2. Their sensory acuity is trained to *immediately calibrate* when they have the response they want.

3. They have the *immediate behavioral flexibility* to vary what they're doing to *achieve the outcome* they want when what they're doing isn't working.

Okay, you have learned something in this chapter. *NOW* it's time to think how you can put this new power into practice. The crucial thing is to write down your intention to use this new knowledge.

Answer these questions: "What are some of the many ways that I can already use and *apply this* in the real world?" and "How can I begin immediately to *use this information* in the real world to cause myself to rapidly *make more money NOW*?"

Write here some of the many ways you are going to immediately use this knowledge to *make more money NOW*:

_____

_____

_____

_____

_____

_____

_____

_____

Note: Exercises for this chapter can be found in Part II, Section A.

Within rapport, <u>anything</u> is possible; out of rapport, <u>nothing</u> is possible.
—Alvin G. Donovan III

CHAPTER 4

Verbal and Psychological Rapport

Benefits of this Chapter
Rapport on the Verbal and Psychological Level: Representational Systems
When You Want to be Powerfully Persuasive
How to Mirror Verbal Responses
Pacing Moods, Opinions and Beliefs
The Steps to Bonding

BENEFITS OF THIS CHAPTER:

- *Understand the language the brain uses to communicate with itself.*
- *Use representational systems to gain even deeper rapport.*
- *Increase your flexibility in being able to "talk the other person's language."*
- *Greatly lower resistance to your thoughts and ideas.*
- *Understand what the eyes tell us about the way a person thinks and speaks.*
- *Learn why to avoid "active listening" and what to do instead.*
- *How pacing and leading works at a deeper level to achieve what you want.*
- *Acquire additional verbal techniques you can use to instantly establish deeper rapport.*

RAPPORT ON THE <u>VERBAL</u> AND <u>PSYCHOLOGICAL</u> LEVEL: REPRESENTATIONAL SYSTEMS

What are our representational systems?

Our representational systems create a map or model of reality for us. This reality is very individual. As information comes into our brain, it does so through one or more of our representational systems. They are:

1. *Visual (V)*—what we see
2. *Auditory(A)*—what we hear
3. *Kinesthetic (K)*—what we feel
4. *Criteria List (CL)*—what we think, how we make sense of our surroundings
5. *Gustatory/Olfactory(G/O)*—what we taste and smell

They are called representational systems because these five senses represent reality to us inside our own heads. Weird as it may seem, we don't operate on "pure reality," that is, on what's really out there. Instead we operate on our map or model of "reality." That model is based on how we perceive and store the information our senses deliver to us—in other words on how we represent the information to ourselves, information that's constantly flowing into our brains through our senses. Since the initial representation of reality coming through our five senses is received through our individual *emotional filters*, the reality we represent to ourselves is pushed even further from actual reality. Everyone has emotional filters fixed more or less permanently in their brains by their early experiences and their culture.

Thus, the entire population of the world consists of individuals communicating with themselves in a sort of code. When you can ***unlock this code,*** they will believe you understand them. And, in fact, you will be understanding them better.

When you match someone's way of coding information verbally by using words from the representation system they are using at the time, they don't have to re-code what you said into the system that makes sense for them.

Also, you assist the person to attain the next step of their process by keeping out of their way and acknowledging them. As we have understood earlier, the brain uses the five senses to make sense out of the information it picks up, filters, stores, and reassembles.

For the purposes of ***using this information*** to get what you want from other people, it is helpful to use the following representational systems:

- *Visual (seeing)*
- *Auditory (hearing)*
- *Kinesthetic (feeling)*

One other important coding system, the *Criteria List*, is useful when eliciting and developing strategies. Criteria List is a representational system of its own. It has seeing, hearing, or feeling components. It has to do with making sense, forming a logical understanding, grasping patterns, setting or realizing priorities, and so on.

One way to determine when words are Criteria List is to determine whether it could fit into more than one representational system or when the person is making lists of important things. If so, then it's a Criteria List word.

For example: take the word *understand*. Can you understand something you see? Sure. Can you understand something you hear? Sure. How about can you understand something you feel? Sure. Because this word, understand, fits more than one system, it's a Criteria List word. You will learn more about Criteria List in Chapter 6.

Here is a easy way for you to **learn this well.**

Beside each of the phrases below, write a (V) for visual, (A) for auditory, and a (K) for kinesthetic, or (CL) for Criteria List to indicate which representational system is presupposed by the phrase.

I see *NOW*	shakes me up	touches me deeply
too loud for me	brilliant example	branch out
argue with me	pretty picture	solid idea
evaluate criteria	tender moment	chime in
hot idea	understand completely	makes sense
quiet please	soft sell	set our view
an oversight	utter a word	I hear you
rings a bell	observe closely	move back
bright idea	pretty view	tone it down
logical		

Here is a list of representational systems, and some words that fall into each of them. The lists of words are by no means exhaustive.

Visual(V)	Auditory(A)	Kinesthetic (K)	Criteria List (CL)
See	Hear	Feel	Logical
Aim	Say	Sting	Organize
Dark	Talk	Sharp	Express
Sketch	Yell	Fumble	Evaluate
View	Rasp	Cool	Feedback
Glow	Sing	Balanced	Explain
Portray	Babble	Shocking	Ponder
Bright	Whine	Merge	Select
Scan	Tone	Bumpy	Rational
Vision	Boom	Bend	Cooperate
Hazy	Chime	Throw	Interact
Dull	Snore	Rough	Understand
Color	Music	Grab	Teach
Show	Describe	Tension	Reward
Cloudy	Loud	Push	Plan
Watch	Clatter	Reach	Relate
Light	Aloud	Connect	Sense
Reflect	Shrill	Jarring	
Dim	Verbalize	Link	
Observe	Clang	Cram	
Pretty	Squawk	Tackle	

Visible	Debate	Pack
Hide	Utter	Shuffle
Focus	Shriek	Unite
Brilliant	Hiss	Catch
Oversight	Resounding	Strain
Diagram	Tell	Sharp
Look	Discuss	Compress
Picture	Phrase	Warm
Blind	Purr	Shoulder
Clear	Call	Grasp
Zooming	Chant	Stick
Image	Noise	Solid
Foggy	Listen	Shape
Sight	Ring	Hard
Survey	Voice	Soft
Glare	Scream	Handle
Reveal	Sound	Fall
Shine	Shout	Cut
Spotless	Speak	Lift
Draw	Tune	Strain

What do the eyes tell us about the representational systems used?

Another way to naturally understand what representational system someone is using is to be aware of where their eyes move. In general—as you look at a person—when their eyes move up and to the right or left they are seeing pictures, what we call *visually accessing*.

When their eyes move from side to side they are hearing sounds, or ***auditorily accessing.*** When they move their eyes down and to the left they are having feelings, or ***kinesthetically accessing***. When they move their eyes down and to the right they are thinking about what is important to them, or ***Criteria List accessing***.

The brain has these eye movements "hard wired" into its system. However, they are **not** the same for all people everywhere. Sometimes you'll encounter individuals who do the opposite. When they look down and to the right they are accessing kinesthetically; when they look down and left they are accessing their Criteria Lists—thinking about what's important to them.

In real life, it's very elementary to ***elicit these cues*** from people by asking certain pre-supposition questions. That is, to see someone visually accessing, you might as, "What color is your car?" and notice the various eye movements they employ as they respond. You can ask someone to "remember the words to your favorite song," and they will move their eyes to the left or right.

You can ask someone, "What does it feel like to be in a really hot bath?" and they will move their eyes down and to the right or left.

Lastly, you can ask someone to "think about what is important to you in life," and they will move their eyes down and to the left or right.

What is the use of this information?

Begin training your brain to immediately notice these sequences of subtle eye movements and words they use (i.e. visual, hearing, or feeling) and, based on those, to respond with the appropriate choice of sequences of representational systems. That's right—you mirror the types of words they use as well as their eye movement clues to establish even deeper rapport. So, if you notice someone's eyes are looking up and to the left or right, you would use visual words such as, "I see." If someone's eyes are looking from side to side, you would use hearing words such as, "I hear you."

Carry this further. If someone uses visual words like, "It looks pretty," respond with something visual, something about color for example, or even, "I see."

In fact, what you also do is watch and listen for the sequence of the representations they go through. For example, when they visually access, then auditory access and then kinesthetically access right after that, what you want to do is to mirror that sequence back in what you say to them. You would use a visual word followed by a auditory word followed by a kinesthetic word, i.e., "Look, I hear that you feel ..." When you *do this well* you will convince the other person to do *what you want*.

Personal Training Tip #5:

> *Within rapport, <u>anything</u> is possible; out of rapport, <u>nothing</u> is possible.*

WHEN YOU WANT TO BE POWERFULLY PERSUASIVE

Keep this process firmly in mind as you go into situations where you need all the persuasive power you can pull together.

Here's a six-step System guaranteed to *make your message irresistible* by putting you into deep rapport:

1. **Always have a clearly visualized outcome-** Make sure you always *have an outcome* clearly in mind when *using these techniques.* Doing this not only makes your aim sharper, it also prevents you from falling prey to the rapport you have created.

2. **Go inside-** When you are deeply in rapport and you *pay attention* to how you feel inside, *begin to realize* that how you feel inside is how they are feeling inside also. Make sure you *use this insight*, and begin to naturally *achieve your outcome*.

What you can do is to go deeply into rapport with the other person and to proceed to put yourself into a state of extreme desire and/or excitement. To do this you can think of the time in your life when you were the most desirous or excited as you have ever been. Amplify that feeling and increase it 10 times *NOW* and the person you are talking with will also begin to feel the same way.

3. **Go deeper into rapport-** Mirror more behaviors, attitudes, beliefs, representational systems, and so on. Make your movements at the same time they do. (Lead up to this.)

4. **Test for rapport before you go for the clincher-** To test for rapport: change your behavior. When they follow you, you are in rapport and may lead them to your outcome. If not, go back *NOW* and get them.

5. **Make your message irresistible- When you mirror the person's rapport controls— predicates, physiology, voice, rate of speech, and rate of breathing—your message becomes <u>irresistible</u> because it's like their own <u>unconscious</u> speaking to them.**

6. **Total honesty required-** All of this will truly only work when employed with total honesty, integrity and congruence. Your product or service must actually be the right one and of benefit to the client. It must be a win-win situation for both of you for this System to work.

Also, bear in mind that dissatisfied customers are likely to badmouth you to a hundred people whereas satisfied clients usually praise you to about half a dozen people.

How to Mirror Verbal Responses

Can you *NOW understand* why techniques like "active listening" don't work for our purposes? If your answer was that a person is precise about what they say based on the way they organize their representational systems, you were right.

Here is an even easier way to *make sure* you begin immediately to *use the right representational system*. This technique is rather similar to active listening; however, it differs in one significant way. Instead of paraphrasing someone else's words, *you say the exact words they say.*

Here's how you do it: you simply *choose some of the words* the person says and *say them back*. This needs to be *done artfully* or you will offend the person. When you merely parrot every word they say, they'll think you're mocking them. However, when *used with subtlety*, this is *very powerful*. Another great side benefit occurs when what you say back will reinforce the thought in the other person's mind.

Use this technique carefully, and you will automatically remain in the same representational system as the person you're matching. You'll be able to selectively *reinforce thoughts* you want to emphasize *in their mind*.

Pacing Moods, Opinions, and Beliefs

An extremely effective way of gaining rapport rapidly involves using the **pacing moods technique**. When someone is in a bad mood you want to pace that mood and then gently lead them out of it.

Make sure that you don't compromise yourself when you pace opinions and beliefs. No matter what a person believes, there will always be something about that belief or opinion you can feel comfortable about pacing. Keep searching until you find that comfortable zone; it can be made to work even when it's only a small part of the entire opinion or belief expressed by the other person.

BONDING

This **major** "pre-wired" human need exists in everybody; we were all born with it.

As a normal process most people seek bonding all the time because the experience of bonding is one of life's most fulfilling experiences. The few who have an aversion to bonding tend to be loners ranging from the socially inept to dangerous psychopaths.

How do we know we're bonding with someone? Simply compare your current feeling to the "bonded feeling."

Familiarity and sameness in terms of beliefs, attitudes, and **values** (**Criteria List**) all help to achieve bonding.

People often don't realize when bonding is happening, they only realize it after the bond is formed. While people usually are unaware of being bonded, they are normally aware of the dis-ease (uneasiness) and distress of being in an *un*bonded condition.

WHAT ARE THE SEVEN STEPS TO BONDING?

Being an instinctive process, bonding often takes place even though the people involved have little or no conscious understanding of the process. This is all well and good for muddling through life. However, for people who want to set high goals, and achieve their desired outcomes as frequently and fully as possible, it's vital to not only have a clear understanding of how the process works, but also to be able to bring it about on demand. Here are the seven steps:

1. **Achieve-** Achieve very deep rapport first.

2. **Attentiveness and responsiveness-** Be attentive and responsive to them and their needs. Make them feel that you really care about their needs.

3. **Confess-** Make appropriate confessions such as, "I'm not perfect. I've gone through a lot of tough times too."

4. **Emote-** Show appropriate emotion in appropriate ways at appropriate times. You must show them your heart. Show them you love them and then you are invincible. Let them experience something of the real you and take a piece of you away with them.

5. **Fall-** Fall in love with them on an **unlimited** and **unconditional** basis. Tell and demonstrate that you love them. However, you must do these things genuinely and with congruence.

6. **Confide-** Use examples from your real life. Multiple examples *intensify the bonding* and will give them the most profound experience ever and completely change their lives.

7. **Amaze-** Amaze yourself. *Do it* (that is, do these steps) with your clients *NOW* and *become amazed* at the results.

You have already come to grips with the idea of mirroring, and with practice you'll easily put this potent System to work in your daily routine. These skills you are able to *learn quickly*.

We recommend focusing on doing just one thing a day over and over again until it becomes second nature. When you *use these techniques* in your daily life and *use them frequently* in your interactions you will *become more successful*. As that happens, obviously you will easily and naturally begin immediately to *make more money NOW*.

Okay, you have learned something in this chapter. *NOW* it's time to think how you can put this new power into practice. The crucial thing is to write down your intention to use this new knowledge.

Answer these questions: "What are some of the many ways that I can already use and *apply this* in the real world?" and "How can I begin immediately to *use this information* in the real world to cause myself to rapidly *make more money NOW?*"

Write here some of the many ways you are going to immediately use this knowledge to *make more money NOW*:

_____

_____

_____

_____

Note: Exercises for this chapter can be found in Part II, Section A.

"People are strategies waiting to be discovered."
—Meg Northcroft

CHAPTER 5

Strategies

Benefits of this Chapter
Strategies
Process Versus Content
General Strategy Elicitation and Employment
Convincer Strategy Elicitation and Employment
How to Get Someone to Make an Instant Decision to Agree
with Your Proposal, or to Buy What You're Selling

BENEFITS OF THIS CHAPTER

- *Learn how to easily discover the other person's decision-making strategy.*
- *Discover how the other person prefers to be persuaded.*
- *Acquire the 7-Step System to discover and employ someone's strategy.*
- *Get others to agree (or to buy) instantly.*
- *Establish and use the other's decision-making process to get them to do what you want.*
- *Grasp the vital difference between process and content.*
- *Gain the skill of using convincer strategy.*
- *Position others in "agreement readiness."*

STRATEGIES

Strategies are the particular sequence of internal and external representations—i.e. seeing (visual), hearing (auditory), feeling (kinesthetic), and making sense of (Criteria List)—leading to a specific outcome. Human experience is an endless series of representations. To deal with this endless sequence more easily, it's useful to classify them in terms of the desired outcomes.

Each individual has different strategies for different situations. Some major categories of strategies are **excellence, decision, learning, motivation, buying** and **convincer**.

The key to all successful persuasion is being able to "aim" or "sequence" your message at the person you are persuading in such a way that they can't say no because **it's what they are already doing all of the time.**

People have a naturally developed resistance to being persuaded to some new decision, belief, policy, or purchase. So, your job is to elegantly present whatever you say in a way that blows right by any resistance.

In fact, your purpose is to make the person salivate to hear more and take action on what you say because **it's how they normally do it all the time**.

After all, who normally likes to say no to themselves?

Strategies:

> *As used in these pages, strategies means the particular sequence of internal and external representations i.e. seeing (visual), hearing (auditory), feeling (kinesthetic), and making sense of (Criteria List) leading to a specific outcome. Human experience is an endless series of representations.*

PROCESS VERSUS CONTENT

To cause persuasion peak performance enhancement quickly, learn to think, talk, and write in terms of process, not content. This is a vital step in immediately becoming highly successful at persuasion.

Think of it this way: Process is the direction and the movement; content is the method of travel. When you spend all of your time concentrating on your method of travel, obviously, you won't go very far.

Questions such as, "What caused…?" and, "How did you decide to…?" will get you process information. The best ways to ***uncover process-oriented information*** are to ***listen for it with your ears and look for it with your eyes*** as the person you are persuading talks. ***They give it to you left and right.***

In fact, they have to give you their strategies because it's what they're doing all the time. With practice, a person's strategies will be as obvious to you as their name, or the clothes they're wearing.

For influencing purposes, the more you *refer to their strategy* and *link it to your proposal,* persuasive purpose, product or service, the more readily you will get what you want from the other person.

Here's an example of an easy and natural way to immediately discover the person's process:

Discover the procedure they use to go from start to finish when they make a decision.

Try this one on for size:

> "First, I organize a list of the important criteria I want from this product. Then, I look at the models available and talk to several people. By this point I have a gut feeling about whether I should go ahead or not."

Look at this in two perspectives. *One,* from the position of what are the overall global aspects to this person's process—such as first, s/he lists criteria, second, s/he looks at the models available, and so on. **Two,** analyze it from the perspective of the order in which s/he organized their representational systems—i.e. visual, auditory, kinesthetic, and Criteria List. The order might run such as this: first s/he used the Criteria List representation, second, s/he looked …and so on.

List the steps here the person goes through on a global level to make a decision:

List the representational systems by code (V, A, K, or CL) the person goes through in order to make a decision:

1. _____   1. _____
2. _____   2. _____
3. _____   3. _____
4. _____   4. _____

The idea is to mirror back the person's exact strategy in the exact sequence they gave it to you. *NOW* calibrate. Let the accurate cycle be the beginning of your **PPP**[1] and keep cycling through their strategy (linked with what you want them to do) over and over again until the person has an overwhelming desire to do as you wish and you achieve your outcome.

For the example above, you can say:

> "Well, to be sure I understand you, you first have a <u>list of important criteria</u> that needs to be met. Next, you want to <u>see</u> the available models. Then you want to <u>speak</u> to several people. By that time, you will have a <u>feeling</u> to do it or not."

Then you would review that person's <u>Criteria List</u> and how your product meets that set of needs. Next you would <u>show</u> them the models, and you would allow them to <u>talk</u> to satisfied customers. The next step is to give them the <u>feeling</u> of ownership.

So you link their strategy with what you want them to do by saying your words following their representation systems sequence (that is, Criteria List words, seeing words, hearing words, feeling words), using PPPL, PPL, PL-LL (this is explained in detail in chapter 8) until you get the deal.

---

[1] PPP stands for Pace, Pace, Pace, the technique of mirroring the other person's actions. You read about it in Chapters 7 & 8, and you'll see more about this vital system in later chapters. Pacing is mentioned here to show you how to combine strategy utilization with it.

7-STEP GENERAL STRATEGY ELICITATION AND EMPLOYMENT SYSTEM

1. Determine your desired outcome and use the New Outcome Generator.

2. Establish rapport.

3. Ask basic questions: "How do you decide ...? "How do you know ...? "What happens first?" and so on.

4. Use all the accessing cues the person gives you: Look with your eyes and listen with your ears. Calibrate.

5. Elicit the major representational systems until complete.

6. Get all the details about the person's Criteria List.

7. Keep cycling through their representational systems and Criteria List (linked with what you want them to do) repeatedly until you truly ***achieve your outcome.***

CONVINCER STRATEGY ELICITATION AND EMPLOYMENT

This is the process one goes through in one's mind in order to become convinced. Once you know it and ***use the process*** and link it with your product, service or proposal, **they will join your cause, contribute to your project, or buy your product/proposal/service.**

Here's how *it works*:

I) Ask "How do you know when you have found an X (fill in the context) that you will Y (fill in the context)?"

For example, "How do you know when an you have found an investment that you will buy (or sell)? What is the procedure you go through from start to finish?"

You will get one of five answers:

1. see

2. hear

3. read about

4. do or feel

5. Criteria List

II) Then ask, "How many times to you need to X (ie. see, hear, read about, do or feel) to *convince yourself*?"

You will get one of four answers:

1. Number of times

2. Length of time

3. Automatic response—right away.

4. Consistent response—each time.

NOW you mirror their exact sequence or strategy and calibrate—take a mental picture. Let the correct mirroring be your first PPP (as explained in Chapter 8) and keep cycling through their strategy repeatedly until you achieve your outcome. For example, someone might say, "To really convince myself, I need to <u>read</u> the information two or three times, then I <u>talk</u> to a few references, and by then I have a <u>feeling</u> whether it's right for me."

You would have them <u>read</u> the information a few times, and after that you would allow them to <u>talk</u> to a few references, and by then they would have a <u>feeling</u> of being convinced. You link their strategy with what you want them to do by saying your words following their representation systems sequence of see, hear, feel.

Also, you would use the PPPL, PPL, PL, LL (as explained in Chapter 8) pattern throughout your presentation.

Personal Training Tip #6:

> *CONVINCER STRATEGY:*
> *A) How do you know when X ?*
> *B) How many times to convince yourself ?*

HOW TO GET SOMEONE TO MAKE AN INSTANT DECISION TO AGREE WITH YOUR PROPOSAL, OR TO BUY WHAT YOU'RE SELLING

According to our research, people store good decisions in a certain part of their brain. To discover where someone stores good decisions, you look where they focus their eyes. When thinking about past good decisions they have made, their eyes will focus on a certain spot in the space in front of them. The place where they focus their eyes we call their "good convincer spot." Then you present your argument, your product, proposal, brochure, or agreement to that "good convincer spot." This procedure causes the other person to believe that what you have presented is a good decision to do, agree to, vote for, or whatever. Personal Training Tip #7, coming up next, tells you how to do it:

Personal Training Tip #7:

> *"GOOD CONVINCER SPOT"*
> *Ask "When have you looked at something and known it was absolutely right for you, known it was the perfect thing for you, and you have been right about it through the years?"*
> *Watch where they focus their eyes and present your product at that "good convincer spot."*
> *Hint: You might need to ask, "What was it?"*

Okay, you have learned something in this chapter. *NOW* it's time to think how you can put this new power into practice. The crucial thing is to write down your intention to use this new knowledge.

Answer these questions: "What are some of the many ways that I can already use and *apply this* in the real world?" and "How can I begin immediately to *use this information* in the real world to cause myself to rapidly *make more money NOW?*"

Write here some of the many ways you are going to immediately use this knowledge to *make more money NOW*:

_____

_____

_____

_____

_____

Note: Exercises for this chapter can be found in Part II, Section A.

CHAPTER 6

Criteria List

Benefits of this Chapter
Understanding and Using Criteria List Representation
The Criteria Lists

BENEFITS OF THIS CHAPTER

- *Learn to establish and use what drives a person to take action so you can motivate others to do what you want.*
- *Learn the function of Criteria List in effective persuasion.*
- *Be able to tailor your presentation to what the other person needs.*
- *Understand how to use a persons Criteria List to eliminate his or her objections to your persuasive purpose.*
- *Acquire the skill of using Criteria List to move a person toward rather than away from your outcome.*

UNDERSTANDING AND USING CRITERIA LIST REPRESENTATION

Would it be helpful to know and use what drives the person you are persuading to *take action*? Achieving great success with your persuasion efforts requires learning how to unpack and use a persons Criteria List.

Using this information will allow you to "customize" everything you say so that it will have the maximum effect on that person-right then. The reason this works is easily explained: Criteria List representation is what we use to "test" something to determine whether or not it's a good decision. That is to say, in order for a person to make a decision to do something, they have a "List" of important "Criteria" which <u>must</u> be met for them to be motivated to *take action*.

Here's how to find out what that Criteria List is for the person you're talking to. Ask this question to explore the person's Criteria List:

"What is important about ... (fill in as suits the situation) for you?"

Examples:

1. "What is important about investments to you?"

2. "What is important about improving your influence skills?"

3. "What is important about an X you'll buy?"

4. "What is important about your job?"

THE CRITERIA LIST

It's what a person uses to decide whether something is a good or bad proposition on the ballot, a good or bad policy, a good or bad purchase for him or her. As people cycle through their decision-making process, their Criteria List **must** be met for them to make a yes decision. The Criteria List, unique to each individual, is what **drives** a person to *take action* or to avoid it.

The more closely your product or service matches the Criteria List of the person you're persuading, the more impact you'll have.

For influencing purposes, the more you *refer to their Criteria List* and *link it to your proposal,* persuasive purpose, product or service, the more readily you will get what you want from the other person.

Criteria List, properly used, can eliminate <u>any</u> objection. However, you do not stop there. Once you get the answer to the above question, you *ask it repeatedly* until you get a "hierarchy" or Criteria List of value information that will absolutely *stun you* as to its effectiveness.

Fill in the blanks with your Criteria List for learning this information.

1. _____Most important

2. _____

3. _____

4. _____Least important

THE FUNCTION OF CRITERIA LIST

All Criteria List serves to move a person towards an objective or away from a problem. This is called, for simplicity the Toward/Away From pattern. It's the basis for all motivation.

- **Toward-** includes such words as Attain, Achieve, Goals, Include, Accomplish, Solutions. Those are what you will hear when a person's Criteria List is moving them toward action of some sort.

- **Away from-** includes words and phrases such as Avoid, Get Away From, Evade, Exclude. Those are what you'll hear when a person's Criteria List is moving them away from action.

Ask this question determine whether a person is moving toward or away from:

"What will having (name their Criteria List) do for you?"

Examples of *move toward* answers:

1. Q. What will having a passive income do for you?

   A. It will enable me to buy more of what I want.

2. Q. What will having high quality do for you?

   A. It makes me feel good knowing that I can afford the best.

3. Q. What will having superior influence skills do for you?

   A. It makes accomplishing all my goals easier and faster.

Examples of *move away from* **answers:**

1. Q. What will having a passive income do for you?

    A. It makes sure I won't have to work when I get older.

2. Q. What will having high quality do for you?

    A. It guarantees me that what I buy won't break down.

3. Q. What will having superior influence skills do for you?

    A. When I have superior influence skills, I won't get told no as often.

NOW, mirror the exact Criteria List words they give you one time to calibrate that you have it. Take a picture. Let the mirroring of their Criteria List be your first PPP (as explained in Chapter 8) and link their Criteria List to what you want them to do. Keep cycling through the person's Criteria List (and link it to what you want them to do) repeatedly until you *achieve your outcomes*.

Personal Training Tip #8:

Criteria List:

What is important to you about X?

What is important about that?

Because?

What will having that do for you? (Towards/Away).

NOTE: With Criteria List words, it's vital to mirror exactly <u>how</u> the person says them, using the exact tone of voice, inflection, speed, and so on that they employ.

Okay, you have learned something in this chapter. *NOW* it's time to think how you can put this new power into practice. The crucial thing is to write down your intention to use this new knowledge.

Answer these questions: "What are some of the many ways that I can already use and *apply this* in the real world?" and "How can I begin immediately to *use this information* in the real world to cause myself to rapidly *make more money NOW?*"

Write here some of the many ways you are going to immediately use this knowledge to *make more money NOW*:

_____

_____

_____

_____

Note: Exercises for this chapter can be found in Part II, Section A.

CHAPTER 7

Presuppositions:
How to *Use Them* for
Greater Persuasive Power

Benefits of this Chapter
Putting the Five Categories of Presuppositions to Work
Adverb/Adjective
Awareness
Time/Number
Spatial
Cause and Effect
"Quotes"
The Design and Construction of Sentences Using Presupposition Power
The Eight Most Dangerous Words

BENEFITS OF THIS CHAPTER

- *Using how the brain processes and understands language.*
- *Obtaining your desired results from "no" responses.*
- *Choosing your language for optimum impact.*
- *Putting the other person into an "agreeing" state.*
- *Knowing what not to say.*

Would it be helpful to speak/write in way such that it puts others in a persuadable condition? Would it be helpful to speak/write in a pattern that causes people to unconsciously say yes? Would it be helpful to speak/write in a manner to cause them to believe whatever you say?

This one chapter has so much power-packed information in it that when you just begin to **master this** part of the book, you will already begin to experience such a **significant leap** in your persuasion abilities that you will **consider this book entirely worthwhile,** even if this is all you learned from it.

For the most part, this chapter deals with the power of a linguistic pattern which **forces the listeners´ subconscious** to accept as true, concepts, ideas and assertions that aren't necessarily stated **directly.**

In other words, what makes them *so* powerful is that everything you want the other person to do is presupposed.

The person **must accept** the basic fundamental principles of what you are saying in order to **make sense** of the sentence.

NOTE: Presuppositions are the most powerful language patterns because your brain processes and understands language by presupposition.

The way you *place them* in the sentence is of utmost importance because everything that follows these words in the sentence is presupposed in the sentence. The mind then has to *accept everything* that follows as true in order to make sense of the sentence. It eliminates resistance and *installs suggestions very profoundly* in the *listener's subconscious.*

It will set the direction for their experience!

So, what are those words, you ask yourself.

Here they are!

- Naturally
- Easily   **Adverb/Adjective**
- Unlimited

- Aware
- Realize(ing)   **Awareness**
- Experience(ing)

- Before
- During   **Time/Number**
- After

- Among
- Expand   **Spatial**
- Beyond

- And/as
- Causes   **Cause and Effect**
- Because

PUTTING THE FIVE CATEGORIES OF PRESUPPOSITIONS TO WORK

You'll note that the words are grouped into five categories, as named above on the right. These are just some of the many examples of each of the categories that make up the most powerful words for persuasion.

We'll start with the *Adverb/Adjective* pattern. Here's a strategy for beginning to easily and naturally use these words effectively:

NOTE: To use Adverb/Adjective Presuppositions powerfully, *always* put the presupposition words before what you want them to do.

Another key to remember: when you use three presupposition words in the sentence before what you want them to do, their mind cannot go back. This is to say, their unconscious mind will just accept it as true in order to make sense of what you are saying, and they will *act on it*.

So if we say to you at a seminar, "You can already begin immediately to understand some of the many ways that *buying our book* will cause you to *make more money*" NOW, you're going to *buy the book*.

I. *Adverb/Adjective* category
- Naturally
- Easily
- Unlimited

NOTE: Everything that follows one of these words is presupposed in the sentence.

Here are some examples:

1. Have you already discovered how <u>easily</u> you can make the decision to ask your friends to volunteer their help to elect (your candidate), or ***refer your friends*** to our company?

2. Have you asked yourself if the <u>unlimited</u> potential of this information is what is making you so excited ***NOW***?

3. Have you <u>naturally</u> discovered how persuasive you are already becoming?

4. Many people begin <u>naturally</u>, Mr. Williams, to create an idea of owning this just prior to making the decision to ***go ahead with it***.

5. <u>Naturally</u>, you will find more than enough reasons to ***go ahead today*** when you understand even a little bit of what I say next.

NOTE: Put the words that describe in front of what they are describing. This forces powerful pictures into the listener's mind. This is not only powerful and effective in speaking, it is also very effective in writing copy. To easily and quickly *use this power-fully*, it always helps to clearly *determine your outcome first*.

NOW, write three examples below using this pattern. Choose examples you'll take back to the "real world" and ***effectively use***. Clearly ***determine your outcome first***.

1. _____

_____

_____

_____

_____

2. _____

    _____

    _____

    _____

    _____

3. _____

    _____

    _____

    _____

    _____

The three words you have been given in the Adverb/Adjective category are, as you have probably figured out by *NOW*, representative of a whole class of descriptive words that will have this same impact when you *use them frequently*.

Here are more:

some	unlimited	many	begin	easily	naturally
readily	infinitely	all	still	continue	already
repeatedly	usually	finally	most	truly	immediately

NOTE: Pack as many of these words as possible together without sounding too strange!

Here are some examples of this strategy at work:

1. You have probably started to *become aware* of some of the <u>many easily</u> activated yet powerful ways you can <u>readily</u> *use this information*.

2. <u>Naturally</u>, the most <u>readily</u> available and, more importantly, competent person to deal with is me.

3. <u>Finally</u>, the <u>most</u> reliably accurate System of persuasion is within your grasp.

Here's a power-packed one for you:

4. Have you asked yourself recently how many services your present provider (or whomever) should be providing but is not? (pause) Since I brought that up, does it *make you wonder* how much more you could be getting when you buy (or whatever) from us?

When you *use these patterns* in writing, do not pack them together too hard or it will make your writing unclear. In speaking, *pack them in* as much as possible.

II. *Awareness* Category

- Aware
- Realize(ing)
- Experience(ing)

This is one of my personal favorites because **simply saying one of these words makes the person you are persuading start to do the mental process that you brought up.**

These words are **very important** to your persuasion arsenal because, like the Adverb/Adjective words, everything that follows them is presupposed to be true.

Also, these words **force the issue** not of "Will you do X …?" (X being whatever you suggest) but instead push for an answer to a more subtle and persuasive question, **"Are you aware that X …?"**

By the way, as you **gain skill** in using these words, the following scenario will probably never happen. However, if it does, here's what to do:

Let's say you ask this question: "Are you aware that…." and the person you are persuading says, NO. You simply respond with, "OH, not yet, huh?!

Here are some examples of this pattern:

1. Is the <u>*awareness*</u> of the power of these patterns starting to **sink in**?

2. The more you begin to **construct in your mind** the ways you'll be **using these patterns**, the more you'll **begin <u>realizing</u> NOW** the explosively profitable Systems **you NOW possess.**

3. Are you starting to <u>***experience the satisfaction***</u> that contributing to this cause—helping elect our candidate—owning this (product) will bring as I tell you about it?

Of course, you can **combine them** just like the others to continually create truly super power suggestions:

"**Becoming <u>aware</u>** of the potentials of this policy allows you to **start <u>experiencing</u>** *NOW* the inner sense of <u>realizing</u> how completely this program fits your needs."

NOW, write in three examples of this pattern in use.

Clearly **determine your outcome first**.

1. _____

    _____

    _____

    _____

    _____

2. _____
   _____
   _____
   _____
   _____

3. _____
   _____
   _____
   _____
   _____

NOTE: Remember, no pattern is an island! Strength comes from combining as many patterns together as possible.

Of course, you can also combine these words with the Adverb/Adjective group of words for even more impact.

Here's an example:

"Naturally, as you *start realizing* the <u>unlimited</u> ways you can <u>easily</u> *become aware* of how joining this team will help you to <u>truly</u> accomplish your goals more <u>rapidly</u> and effectively, you will start <u>imagining</u> the success you can actually achieve with my help and guidance. *NOW,* are you starting to <u>experience</u> the possibilities?"

Of course, as before, the words I chose are my personal favorites. Here are some additional words in this category that you can also choose from:

realize(ing)	aware	know(ing)	understand(ing)
think(ing)	feel(ing)	wonder(ing)	puzzle(ing)
speculate(ing)	perceive(ing)	discover(ing)	experience(ing)
accomplish(ing)	fulfill(ing)	grasp(ing)	reconsider(ing)
weigh(ing)	consider(ing)	assume(ing)	conceive(ing)

Exercise:

Let's put all this together in an exercise that will help you use powerful combinations.

Write a paragraph using the following presuppositions in the order listed:
- Naturally
- Aware
- Unlimited
- *NOW*
- Experiencing

Write your paragraph here. Clearly *determine your outcome first.*

_____

_____

_____

_____

_____

III. *Time/Number* Category

- Before
- During
- After

These words use some aspect of Time and/or Numbers to create the presuppositions of your choice. The easiest way to define this category is to give some examples:

1. <u>After</u> you *work with me NOW* you'll understand.

2. <u>Before</u> you decide just how easy this decision is to make, let me tell you a few things that might help, okay?

3. <u>During</u> our time together today, could you be applying the benefits you will be discovering about this (product or service) to your life?

NOW write three of your own sentences using this pattern. Make them relevant to your day-to-day business. Clearly, *determine your outcome first.*

1. _____

   _____

   _____

   _____

   _____

2. _____

   _____

   _____

   _____

   _____

3. _____

   _____

   _____

   _____

   _____

And of course, you can *combine all the patterns* together to craft even more exciting suggestions:

4. <u>During</u> our discussion today, <u>naturally</u> you will <u>already</u> <u>begin</u> <u>experiencing</u> excitement about what the future holds for you as you <u>begin</u> to <u>understand</u> how <u>easily</u> leverageable this information is for you.

Here are more words that fit into this category:

before	former	another	current/ly	while
during	after	when	foremost	continue
early	later	until	first/ly	eventually
second/ly	highest	chief	other	more
in addition to	was	earliest	latest	

IV. *Spatial* Category

- Among
- Expand
- Beyond

Spatial words are always used to create some relationship between things. This could be thoughts, ideas, products, services or anything that will help you. These words evoke powerful imagery in the mind of the listener as well. Here are some examples:

1. From <u>among</u> the positive thoughts that you're already starting to realize you have about ***working with our firm***, will come the most obvious, yet overlooked reason to ***bring us on board NOW***. (Of course you see and hear the plethora of additional presuppositions used above, do you not?)

2. To <u>expand</u> on your ever-growing ideas that contain the essence of your good feeling regarding ***using this information*** powerfully, think of the money you will be making.

3. That's a great observation. Let me suggest that as you ***start to experience*** the realization of what you just said, you can begin to realize that the full, positive ramifications will go <u>beyond</u> even your expectations. ***NOW*** can you imagine how much further they will go?

NOW, you write three sentences of your own using this pattern. Clearly ***determine your outcome first***.

1. _____

  _____

  _____

  _____

  _____

2. _____

  _____

  _____

  _____

  _____

3. _____

  _____

  _____

  _____

  _____

Here are some additional words in this category you can also use:

against	along	among	apart from
around	aside from	behind	below
beneath	beyond	along with	down
from	above	without	including
from behind	from under	off	in place of
in	withdraw(ing)	out of	round
short of	through	proceed(ed,ing)	under
uncover	off the top	underlying	touching
close(er)	near(er)	further	expanded
enlarge(ed,ing)	toward	on	undergone
upward(ly)	dissect	cut away	lower
separate			

NOW, put together some statements using the following presupposition words in the order given. Aim at something important; avoid the trivial.

- Realizing
- After
- Beyond
- Easily
- Effectively

Throw in, *"Are you with me?"*

6. *NOW,* realizing

Make some notes here for the above exercise so you can do it. You might want to outline the above. Clearly *determine your outcome first.*

_____

_____

_____

_____

_____

_____

_____

_____

_____

_____

_____

_____

V. The *Cause and Effect* Category is Extremely Powerful!

One of the main reasons this category is so powerful is because it's the natural way that we state our beliefs. Actually this pattern is pivotal to the balance of the book in that it also is the most basic expression of pacing and leading.

Three major benefits contained in this pattern alone are the abilities to:

1. Use a naturally occurring pattern in language to install suggestions.
2. Create "realities" of whatever you want causing whatever else you want.
3. Speak in terms of the way beliefs are organized inside people's minds, therefore, what you say is even more believable.

Here are the words:

- and
- as
- cause
- because

For the sake of making this pattern simple, let's split it up into two distinct groups with And/As being in one group and Cause/Because being in another. Let's start with *Cause/Because*.

The reason this pattern is called cause and effect is because one thing can literally be said to cause another. The pattern is used simply just as it is written. It basically takes on the pattern of, X (pace) happens and automatically then, Y (lead) happens.

Employ these rules to make the pattern simple:

- Generally, **X** is a pace (truism, true, or verifiable).

- Generally, **Y** is a lead (what you want them to do, believe, your outcome).

- Most importantly, ANY **X** Can CAUSE ANY **Y** !!!

Here are some examples:

1. Sitting there <u>causes</u> you to ***completely absorb*** what I am saying. And, as you ***completely absorb it***, it will <u>cause</u> you to ***immediately accept it*** at the ***deepest levels***.

2. Thinking your next thought <u>causes</u> you to ***agree with me*** that you need to really ***master this material***.

3. Simply saying that excuse <u>causes</u> you to understand why you already don't believe it.

Isn't this a neat pattern?

"QUOTES"

Another pattern that you can use with any of the five categories is called "Quotes." This pattern works so well because you can literally say anything you want to say and just say that you are quoting someone else.

Here's an example:

I was talking with a client the other day and she said, "The effectiveness of your material is so profound that you must be loaded with clients- I mean, just listening to what you say would <u>cause</u> anybody to ***get excited*** and ***decide on the spot*** to bring you in, when they really want to ***make more money NOW.***"

This kind of excitement is justified when you consider I helped her increase her income last month by $25,000.

THE DESIGN AND CONSTRUCTION OF SENTENCES USING PRESUPPOSITION POWER

The following takes you through the step-by-step design and construction of a cause and effect sentence using the template provided.

Step 1 is to *determine your outcome.* We have determined that you have excellent learning.

Step 2 is to fill in the leads, which we have done in the box in the top row.

Step 3 is to fill in the paces, which we have done in the second row.

Step 4 is to fill in the cause and effect connectors which we have done in the third row.

Next you see the result: **Doing this exercise causes excellent learning.**

The following template is blank. You are to design three different sentences that you can use in the real world using this structure and format. Make it something you can use in the real world to *make more money NOW*.

Pace = True, Truism, Verifiable   C/E = Cause/Effect   Lead = Your Outcome

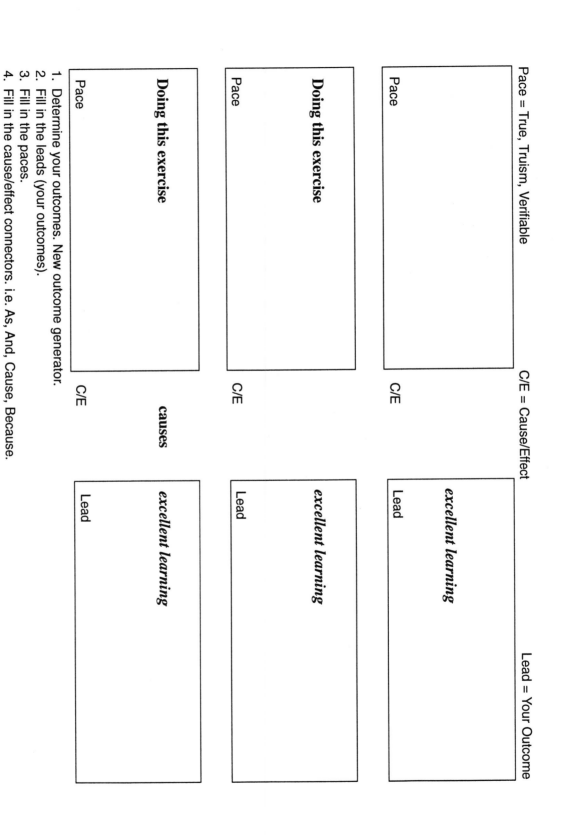

Pace

C/E

excellent learning

Lead

Doing this exercise

Pace

C/E

excellent learning

Lead

Doing this exercise

Pace

C/E

causes

excellent learning

Lead

1. Determine your outcomes. New outcome generator.
2. Fill in the leads (your outcomes).
3. Fill in the paces.
4. Fill in the cause/effect connectors. i.e. As, And, Cause, Because.

82

Doing this exercise causes *excellent learning.*

(See how easy it is!!?)

Pace = True, Truism, Verifiable   C/E = Cause/Effect   Lead = Your Outcome

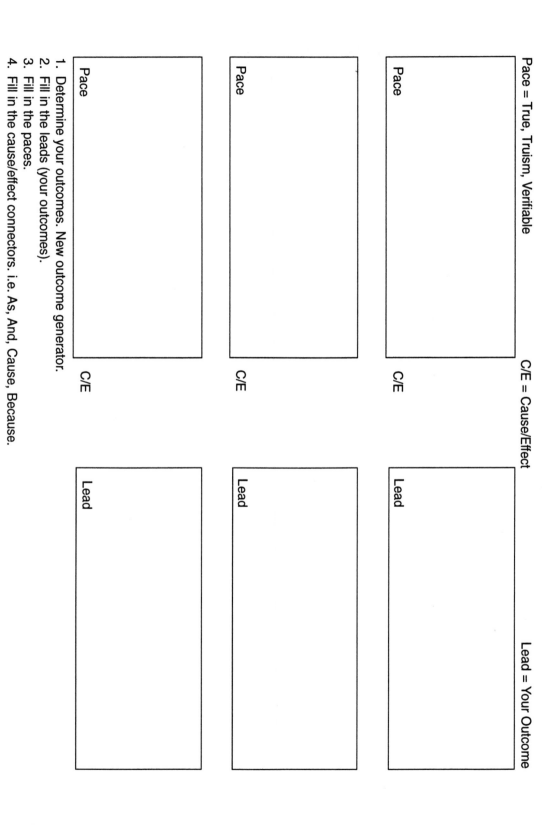

Pace   C/E   Lead

Pace   C/E   Lead

Pace   C/E   Lead

1. Determine your outcomes. New outcome generator.
2. Fill in the leads (your outcomes).
3. Fill in the paces.
4. Fill in the cause/effect connectors. i.e. As, And, Cause, Because.

Implied Cause and Effect: Implied cause and effect takes advantage of two vital words: *And*, and *As*.

This pattern simply implies that two things are linked together. The basic pattern is, As X (pace) happens, Y (your lead) naturally follows.

Here are a few examples of this pattern in action:

1. <u>As</u> you *learn this pattern* and start to *use it well*, you will have a certain sense of accomplishment.

2. <u>As</u> you start to *assimilate this information,* you will instantly begin to find ways to *use it*.

3. *NOW,* <u>as</u> the realization begins to *sink in* of how easily, rapidly and efficiently *your profits* will *go up* as a result of using my help, naturally, you'll get *more and more excited!*

Here are some more selections to broaden your Cause and Effect word base:

Kindles	Brings to pass	Generates	Allows	Since
Causes	Forces(e)	Makes	Invokes	Settles
Creates	Stimulates	Verifies	Justifies	Determines
Proves	Constitutes	Permits	Because	And/As

Follow these steps:

- Clearly *determine your outcome first*.
- Fill in the leads (your outcomes).
- Fill in the paces.
- Fill in cause-effect connectors.

NOTE: The following takes you through the step-by-step design and construction of a sentence using the templates provided. Next you see the resulting sentence. The next template is blank. You are to design three different sentences which you can use in the real world using this structure and format. Make it something you can use in the real world to *make more money NOW*.

Pace = True, Truism, Verifiable   C/E = Cause/Effect   Lead = Your Outcome

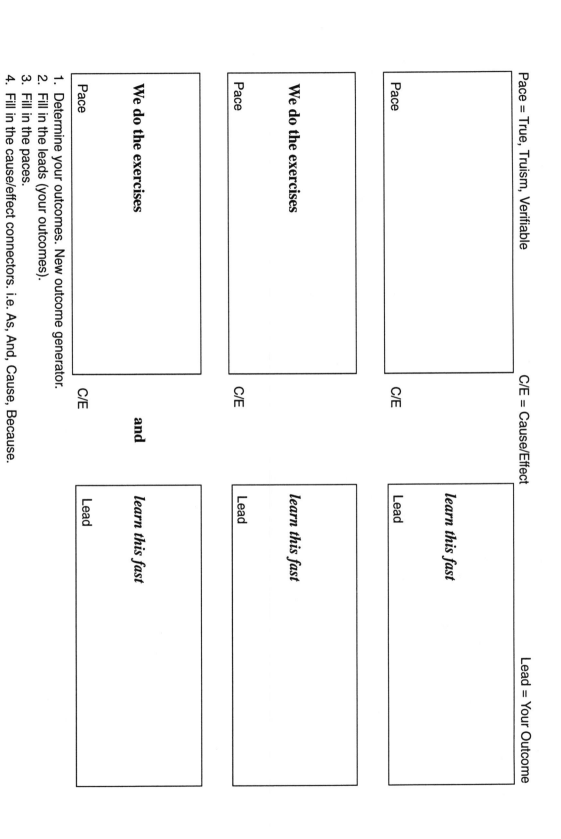

Pace

learn this fast

C/E

Lead

We do the exercises

Pace

learn this fast

C/E

Lead

We do the exercises

Pace

and

learn this fast

C/E

Lead

1. Determine your outcomes. New outcome generator.
2. Fill in the leads (your outcomes).
3. Fill in the paces.
4. Fill in the cause/effect connectors. i.e. As, And, Cause, Because.

We do the exercises and *learn this fast*.

(See how easy it is!!)

Pace = True, Truism, Verifiable   C/E = Cause/Effect   Lead = Your Outcome

Pace

C/E

Lead

Pace

C/E

Lead

Pace

C/E

Lead

1. Determine your outcomes. New outcome generator.
2. Fill in the leads (your outcomes).
3. Fill in the paces.
4. Fill in the cause/effect connectors. i.e. As, And, Cause, Because.

Okay, *NOW* you have presuppositions for persuasion. *Practice them constantly* and you will be well rewarded for your efforts.

THE NINE MOST DANGEROUS WORDS (AND PHRASES)

Eliminate them! Purge them from your vocabulary NOW!

1. But

2. Try

3. If

4. Might

5. Would have

6. Could have

7. Should have

8. Can't

9. Why

Here are the reasons these words work against or even defeat persuasion:

But - This word negates anything that was said before. Such as, "I want to help you but ..." This really means, "I don't want to help you." Eliminate *but;* replace it with **and**.

Try - This word presupposes failure. It's a subtle suggestion to fail to do whatever follows. For example, "When you try and get this, it will really benefit you," actually means, "I know you probably won't get to it, but if you did it would benefit you." The only time I would ever suggest you "try" to do something would be in a reverse manner, as in, "When you use this System, try in vain to resist becoming too successful too soon!" and follow this with a chuckle.

If - This word presupposes the person might not. Such as, "If you want to pursue this with me," suggests they might not want to pursue it. *If* is used by people who haven't built a compellingly persuasive message, so they throw their *If* phrase against the wall as a weak close.

Whenever you ever hear yourself using this word *if*, stop and evaluate whether your overall message is weak. You can substitute *before, during, after*, or *when* for the word *if* (depending on the sentence structure and the intended meaning) to make your message more persuasive.

However, there are some times when you can us *if*, as long as doing so doesn't weaken your message. For example, "Have you asked yourself <u>if</u> the unlimited power of this book is what is making you so excited?" In this example, none of the substitutes given above for *if* would make sense.

Might - This word is wishy-washy, maybe yes, maybe no. It says nothing definite. Although it's not a severely negative word, just be sure you don't use it in a way that weakens the power of your message.

Would have, Could have, Should have - These are all past tense phrases and can have a seriously negative impact on your persuasion message. Generally, you want to be leading people into the present time, so they can and will **act NOW**. Often these words create a whining atmosphere as well.

Can't - This word is in a class of words called negations. Negations, used the way most people use them, can pose a serious threat to your persuasion message.

When you say sentences like, "You can't use negations" it forces your mind to first picture using negations, and then in some way negate that picture.

Think back to a time when you saw a mother with her child on a rainy day. As the two of them approach a mud puddle, the mother says, "Mary, don't step in the mud puddle." And what does Mary do? Of course, she jumps right in.

The reason for this is that any negation forces the mind to think about the very thing that you don't want the person you are persuading to do. As you know, one of the most important elements to any persuasion is to get the people you're persuading to make a mental image of doing what you want them to do. Thus, words like can't, create the very image you don't want the person to make. Of course, there are powerful and creative ways of using negation—just be careful to use negation properly or not at all until you become excellent at it through study and practice.

By the way, how could you use negation powerfully when you encounter a polarity response, that is, someone who has a tendency to do the opposite of what you tell them?

You can say to a client, "I'm going to explain a bit about our product (program, policy, whatever you want them to agree to) and don't get too excited too soon." (ha ha!)
Why - Can cause the listener to feel defensive and the answers may prove irrelevant. Always ask how instead and generate the necessary process-rich information.

Okay, you have learned something in this chapter. *NOW* it's time to think how you can put this new power into practice. The crucial thing is to write down your intention to use this new knowledge.

Answer these questions: "What are some of the many ways that I can already use and *apply this* in the real world?" and "How can I begin immediately to *use this information* in the real world to cause myself to rapidly *make more money NOW*?"

Write here some of the many ways you are going to immediately use this knowledge to *make more money NOW*:

_____

_____

_____

Note: Exercises for this chapter can be found in Part II, Section A.

CHAPTER 8

The Single Most Powerful Persuasion Format

Benefits of this Chapter
The Single Most Powerful Persuasion Format
Pacing
Leading
The Format for Pacing and Leading Persuasion

BENEFITS OF THIS CHAPTER

- *Put others into an even more agreeable state.*
- *Compel others to do what you want.*
- *Cause others to say yes to what you're driving at.*
- *Use presuppositions, pacing, and leading to create irresistible messages.*
- *Put others into a persuadable state.*
- *Make others agree with what you're saying.*

THE SINGLE MOST POWERFUL PERSUASION FORMAT

This pattern is so fundamental to all good persuasion that taking the time to really *master it* will pay off hugely for you- in far greater proportion to the time it takes to learn it.

Remember verbal and written pacing and leading?

PACING

Pacing is talking/writing about either what is true and verifiable in a person's ongoing experience or talking/writing about what is commonly accepted as true. Talking about what is commonly accepted as true is also called "using truism."

LEADING

Leading is talking/writing about what you want the other person to believe that as yet is not verified.

THE PACING AND LEADING PERSUASION FORMAT:

- *Pace, Pace, Pace, Lead*
- *Pace, Pace, Lead*
- *Pace, Lead*
- *Lead, Lead (to your outcome)*

NOTE: All of your behaviors including everything that comes out of your mouth is either a pace or a lead, or not. It is up to you to begin to make the decision to elegantly communicate in patterns that are powerful, or not.

Personal Training Tip #9:

> *PPPL*
> *PPL*
> *PL*
> *LL*

Example:

"As you sit there, reading this information, letting your eyes follow each word, you can to **begin to discover** how this information will allow you to **increase your persuasion power.** And as you think about how that might happen, and listen to what those ideas are inside your own thoughts, it may stimulate you to **get excited** at how much easier this makes the process of convincing someone to do what you want. In fact, feeling that excitement begin to **build NOW,** causes you to want to practice, to **perfect this technique.**

This technique is strong enough to get people to go along with whatever you say, so much that the more you *utilize it* the more you will suddenly *make more money NOW*. This enables you to live the lifestyle you desire."

NOW, can you go over the above example and **pick out the paces and leads?**

We are teaching you a way to cause a person to feel compelled to say *yes* to whatever you're saying. One of the main reasons to use pacing and leading is that it automatically sets up a person's unconscious to say *yes* to what you are saying or writing. Also, **when you speak using this pattern, the <u>other</u> person becomes dependent upon <u>you</u> for their next thought or action.**

The way to do so is verbal or written pacing and leading.

What is verbal pacing and leading? It's a sophisticated technique that links things that are true and verifiable with things that you'd like people to believe are true. Here are some examples of things that qualify as **pacing:**

1. You are reading this.

2. You can feel the temperature around you.

3. On the news last night ….

4. As you participate in this learning experience….

5. On my way to see you today, I was thinking….

   What are some of your own?

6. _____

7. _____

8. _____

Those qualified as pacing because they are true and verifiable or qualify as truisms (things that are accepted as true).

Leads are anything you want people to believe. So here are some examples of things that could be considered as leads:

1. You are excited about this information.

2. You are becoming committed to learning more about this.

3. Verbal pacing and leading makes persuasion easier.

4. Verbal pacing and leading creates a lullaby type of effect.

5. This book will have ongoing benefits that you haven't even become aware of yet.

What are some of your own leads? Clearly *determine your outcome first.*

6. _____

7. _____

8. _____

Can you *begin to see* the difference between pacing and leading?

Pacing statements are statements that are *true!* You can't take exception to them! That's what makes them *so powerful* for our purposes.

Leading statements are what you want the person you're persuading to believe. They are not proven necessarily, and they are what you want your prospect to believe.

The following format will assist you in *mastering this technique:*

PACE, PACE, PACE, LEAD

PACE, PACE, LEAD

PACE, LEAD

LEAD, LEAD (to your outcome)

Follow these steps:

a) Determine your outcomes.

b) Fill in the leads (your outcomes).

c) Fill in the paces.

d) Fill in increasingly stronger cause-effect connectors.

e) Fill in with presuppositions.

f) "Mark off" outcomes. (There is more about "marking off" hidden outcome directives in Chapter 9.)

Example:

"As you review what you've read so far and the seconds pass while you *think about this* in your own way, this action allows you to *begin to understand* the value of *using this System* to get more of *what you want* when *you want it.*

And as you *begin to understand* the value of this, thinking back to a time when this might of made a difference can stimulate you to *begin to anticipate* the benefits that will be yours as you begin to *use it.*

While that anticipation *builds NOW,* it causes you to take just a second to *tell yourself* how thrilled you are to have found this at a time when you can really *use it. NOW,* the more that realization begins to sink in perhaps even outside your awareness that the real key to persuasion is having skills like these that you can use the more that causes you to already start to wonder how you will use this to *make more money NOW*."

NOW let's go back over the three paragraphs above and analyze it. First, before we do that, read it one more time. Can you understand how the pacing and leading creates a powerful influence that literally compels your experience? Here are the paces and leads:

Pace—review what you've read.

Pace—the seconds pass.

Pace—while you think about this in your own way.

Lead—understand the value of using this

Pace—understanding the value of using this

Pace—thinking back to a time, might have made a difference.

Lead—anticipate the benefits, use it.

Pace- anticipation builds

Lead- tell yourself how thrilled you are to have found this.

Lead- realization begins to sink in

Lead- the real key to persuasion is having skills like these.

Lead- wonder how you will use this to *make more money NOW*.

Do this. Read just the leads above. Preferably read them aloud. Had those been all that was written, they wouldn't deliver nearly as much persuasive impact as when you have the pacing statements with them.

Each time you read a pace, your unconscious goes "yes." Only this is so subtle—albeit powerful—that nobody thinks of it as an assault. Instead, you have created a comfortable environment, one that supports the other person in moving with you.

Here's another example for you:

"As you sit there reading this information, letting your eyes follow each word, you can *begin to discover* how this information will allow you to *increase your persuasion power*.

And as you think about how that might happen, and listen to what those ideas are inside your own thoughts, it may stimulate you to *get excited* at how much easier this makes the process of convincing someone to do what you want.

In fact, feeling that excitement beginning to *build, NOW,* causes you to want to begin to practice to *perfect this technique.*

This technique is strong enough to get people to go along with whatever you say, so much so that the more you *utilize it* the more you will suddenly *make more money NOW*. You will also be able to live the lifestyle you desire."

NOW, let's see whether you can list the paces and leads in this paragraph.

Pace—

Pace—

Pace—

Lead—

Pace—

Pace—

Lead—

Pace—

Lead—

Lead—

Lead—

Lead—

Also, note that the paragraph begins with an external orientation and moves the reader to an internal orientation, thus further facilitating the persuasion process.

NOTE: The following takes you step by step through the design and construction of a PPL, PPL, PL, LL paragraph using the templates provided. Next you see the result: a paragraph written in PPPL, PPL, PL, LL. Then, the following template is blank and you are to design a PPPL, PPL, PL, LL paragraph using this structure and format. Make it something you can use in the real world to *make more money NOW*.

Pace = True, Truism, Verifiable   C/E = Cause/Effect   Lead = Your Outcome

| Pace | C/E | Pace | C/E | Pace | C/E | Lead |

us to learn this fast

Learning this fast
Last Lead = Pace   C/E | Pace | C/E | Lead |

us to learn this well

We learn this well
Last Lead = Pace   C/E | Lead |

we will use it in the real world

We become more persuasive
Lead   C/E | Your Outcome |

us to make more money now

1. Determine your outcomes. New outcome generator.
2. Fill in the leads (your outcomes).
3. Fill in the paces.
4. Fill in the increasingly stronger cause/effect connectors. i.e. As, And, Since, Allows, Permits, Verifies, Generates, Creates, Stimulates, Kindles, Because, Makes, Proves, Causes.
5. Fill in with presuppositions.
6. "Mark Off" outcomes.

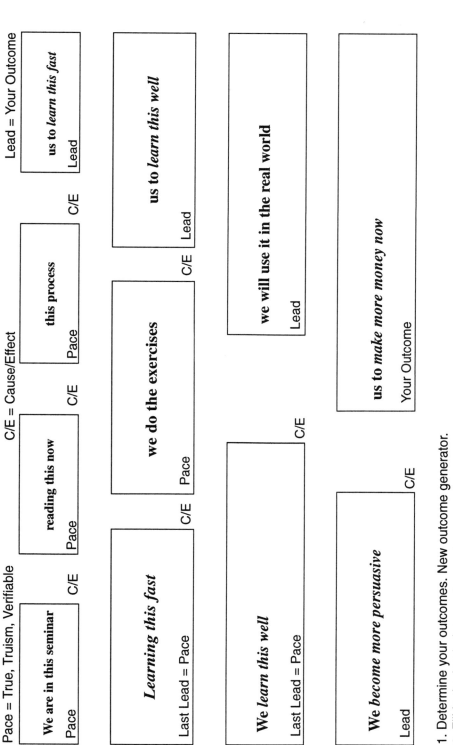

1. Determine your outcomes. New outcome generator.
2. Fill in the leads (your outcomes).
3. Fill in the paces.
4. Fill in the increasingly stronger cause/effect connectors. i.e. As, And, Since, Allows, Permits, Verifies, Generates, Creates, Stimulates, Kindles, Because, Makes, Proves, Causes.
5. Fill in with presuppositions.
6. "Mark Off" outcomes.

Pace = True, Truism, Verifiable   C/E = Cause/Effect   Lead = Your Outcome

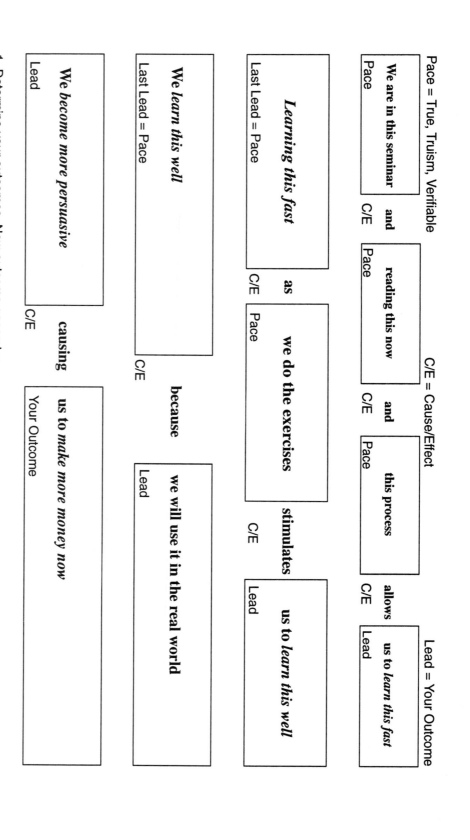

| We are in this seminar | and | reading this now | and | this process | allows | us to *learn this fast* |
| Pace | C/E | Pace | C/E | Pace | C/E | Lead |

| *Learning this fast* | as | we do the exercises | stimulates | us to *learn this well* |
| Last Lead = Pace | C/E | Pace C/E | | Lead C/E |

| *We learn this well* | because | we will use it in the real world |
| Last Lead = Pace | C/E | Lead |

| *We become more persuasive* | causing | us to *make more money now* |
| Lead | C/E | Your Outcome |

1. Determine your outcomes. New outcome generator.
2. Fill in the leads (your outcomes).
3. Fill in the paces.
4. Fill in the increasingly stronger cause/effect connectors. i.e. As, And, Since, Allows, Permits, Verifies, Generates, Creates, Stimulates, Kindles, Because, Makes, Proves, Causes.
5. Fill in with presuppositions.
6. "Mark Off" outcomes.

104

We are in this seminar and reading this *NOW* and this process allows us to *learn this fast. Learning this fast* as we do the exercises stimulates us to *learn this well.*

We *learn this well* because we will *use it* in the real world. We *become more persuasive*, causing us to *make more money NOW.*

(See how easy it is!)

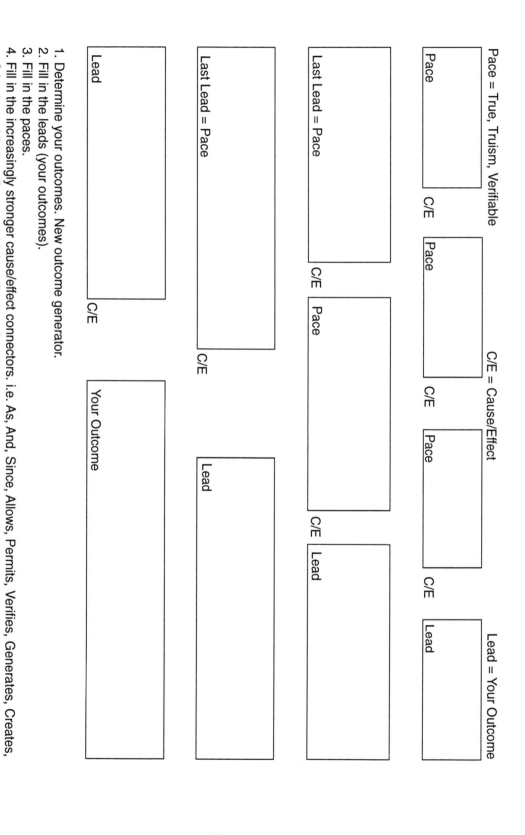

Pace = True, Truism, Verifiable   C/E = Cause/Effect   Lead = Your Outcome

Pace | C/E | Pace | C/E | Pace | C/E | Lead

Last Lead = Pace | C/E | Pace | C/E | Lead

Last Lead = Pace | C/E | Lead | Your Outcome

Lead | C/E

1. Determine your outcomes. New outcome generator.
2. Fill in the leads (your outcomes).
3. Fill in the paces.
4. Fill in the increasingly stronger cause/effect connectors. i.e. As, And, Since, Allows, Permits, Verifies, Generates, Creates, Stimulates, Kindles, Because, Makes, Proves, Causes.
5. Fill in with presuppositions.
6. "Mark Off" outcomes.

106

Personal Training Tip #10:

There are two times in a persuasion opportunity when you __must__ use the PPPL format:

(a) *At the beginning of every persuasion opportunity to set the direction of the encounter.*

(b) *When you repeat back the person's Criteria List and strategy, and get it right, let that be the first Pace, Pace, Pace of the PPPL format. You then go on to use Pacing and Leading to link their strategy and Criteria List with what you want them to do.*

So, for example if someone has the following strategy and Criteria List:

They need to __read__ information 2-3 times. Next they need to __speak__ to several references and then consider a __list of criteria__ that includes the words "__practical__, __good__, __fun__."

You can say, "So, if I understand you correctly, you need to __read__ the information 2-3 times first. (Pace) Next you need to __speak__ to several references (Pace) and then consider if it is __practical__, __good__ and __fun__. (Pace) In that case, that's great (Lead). The reason is that you can __read__ this information several times (Pace) and then you can __speak__ to several references (Pace) who will tell you this is really __practical__ (Lead). I say it's __practical__ (Pace) because it will be __good__ for you (Lead) as well as __fun__ (Lead). So NOW let's go to the next step. (Lead)."

Okay, you have learned something in this chapter. *NOW* it's time to think how you can put this new power into practice. The crucial thing is to write down your intention to use this new knowledge.

Answer these questions: "What are some of the many ways that I can already use and *apply this* in the real world?" and "How can I begin immediately to *use this information* in the real world to cause myself to rapidly *make more money NOW*?"

Write here some of the many ways you are going to immediately use this knowledge to *make more money NOW*:

_____

_____

_____

_____

Note: Exercises for this chapter can be found in Part II, Section A.

CHAPTER 9

Hidden Outcome Directives

Benefits of this Chapter
Hidden Outcome Directives
Analogical Marking

BENEFITS OF THIS CHAPTER

This pattern is one of our personal favorites. It has been responsible for earning us a significant amount of money, and it can do the same for you.

- *How to bypass the conscious filtering system in a person.*
- *Subtly give instructions that will be carried out by the person.*
- *Do your persuading on both an unconscious level and a conscious level.*
- *Dramatically increase your personal power by understanding how to access instant acceptance in the person you are communicating with.*

HIDDEN OUTCOME DIRECTIVES

Hidden outcome directives fit into the structure of a spoken or written sentence without calling attention to their existence. They are the "outcomes" you are "directing" the other person to do and are "hidden" within the sentence.

Example 1:

"When you ***learn this material*** you will be able to ***use it powerfully***, and that will allow you to ***make more money NOW***."

Write the hidden outcome directives down here that are used in the above example.

1. _____ _____

2. _____

3. _____

Notice that when you just read the hidden outcome directives in the example, they make sense on their own. This is communicating in multiple levels.

NOTE: From *NOW* on, whenever <u>you</u> write a hidden outcome directive, underline it. Note the example above. You will notice that throughout the whole book <u>we</u> have used *bold italics* to "mark off" the outcomes we are directing your unconscious mind to follow.

Example 2:

"I'm wondering *by NOW* when you can, John, *feel great inside,* understanding the value of what you have learned so far, and this is just the beginning!"

Write down the hidden outcome directives below:

1. _____

2. _____

In the above example we did several important things that you should be aware of. First, we used the directive *by (buy) NOW*. This is called a phonological ambiguity.

In other words the mind translates that into all the possibilities of what that word sounds like and acts appropriately. So, essentially, what you are doing is to direct or command the person to *buy NOW!* Think then, about what using the word "know" might do in a persuasion presentation.

In the above example we also used what is called a noun substitution. Reread the example above and leave out the name John. The meaning is still same, however adding the name makes the directive stronger because it focuses attention to the person.

You can put the name before or after the hidden outcome directive and still get the same results. You can't use this often (adding someone's name before or after the directive) because it will sound funny. You can *use it* occasionally, though.

Here's a third example for you so you can begin to *understand this even more* as you *read it*.

Example 3:

"I had a client come in the other day and ask me if I thought this would be a good product for him to buy. I told him, 'When you want a good investment, by all means, ***buy it.***' I said, ***'Take my word,*** it will do what you want.' Finally I said, 'You are the only one who can ***convince yourself*** that it's right.' Then I asked if he felt it's right to ***go ahead and get it***. He said it was. I get asked frequently for my advice and I would love to be of service in any way I can."

Write the hidden outcome directives that were used below:

1. _____

2. _____

3. _____

4. _____

NOW, look back over the three examples you were given. Note that they follow a specific format. Each one used a different structure for hidden outcome directives. Example 1 used hidden outcome directives in a sentence format. Example 2 used hidden outcome directives in a question format. Example 3 used hidden outcome directives in a quotation format.

ANALOGICAL MARKING

Analogical marking is a fancy way of describing the way in which hidden outcome directives are marked off verbally or written to ***draw attention to them unconsciously***.

Here are five different methods you can use to *mark off hidden outcome directives*:

*1. Pause before and after giving the hidden outcome directive.

*2. Change your tone (deeper or higher) while giving the hidden outcome directive.

*3. Increase or decrease your volume when giving the hidden outcome directive.

4. Make a specific motion when giving the hidden outcome directive.

5. Use facial expressions or anything else that "marks off" the hidden outcome directive.

* The first three methods, 1, 2 and 3, are the most powerful when used together to mark off a hidden outcome directive.

NOTE: When you say hidden outcome directives the inflection of your voice *goes down* regardless of the sentence structure. That is what makes it *so powerful!*

Think of it this way—most people remember very little of what was said or done. What you ***"mark off"*** often leaves the deepest impression. To ***do this right*** you must ***exaggerate it.***

To effectively ***"mark off"*** hidden outcome directives, really ***exaggerate this action***:

Personal Training Tip #11:

> *A. Pause before and after giving the hidden outcome directive.*
>
> *B. Change your tone (deeper or higher) while giving the hidden outcome directive.*
>
> *C. Increase or decrease your volume when giving the hidden outcome directive.*

Exercise: Choose 5 two-to-four word hidden outcome directives that you will use daily. Write them below. Clearly *determine your outcome first.*

1. _____

2. _____

3. _____

4. _____

5. _____

NOW, use these hidden outcome directives in a statement that consciously does not call attention to them. Write them down here. Underline all hidden outcome directives.

1. _____

2. _____

3. _____

4. _____

5. _____

NOW, use these hidden outcome directives in a question that consciously does not call attention to them. Write them down here. Underline all hidden outcome directives.

1. _____

2. _____

3. _____

4. _____

5. _____

NOW, use these hidden outcome directives in quotes that consciously does not call attention to them. Write them down here. <u>Underline all hidden outcome directives.</u>

1. _____

2. _____

3. _____

4. _____

5. _____

NOW, using what you have learned so far, write one sentence that uses pacing, leading, and several presuppositions, as well as at least two hidden outcome directives. Write the sentence below:

1. _____

_____

_____

_____

_____

Here's yet another way to *use hidden outcome directives powerfully*. You quote yourself talking to yourself in your own head.

Example:

"You know, it's really neat! When I talk to you, I *get excited* about what the possibilities are for the future. I even say to myself, *be open* to really be of service here. I really *appreciate our relationship*!"

Write one example for yourself here.

1. _____

   _____

   _____

   _____

   _____

Okay, you have learned something in this chapter. *NOW* it's time to think how you can put this new power into practice. The crucial thing is to write down your intention to use this new knowledge.

Answer these questions: "What are some of the many ways that I can already use and *apply this* in the real world?" and "How can I begin immediately to *use this information* in the real world to cause myself to rapidly *make more money NOW*?"

Write here some of the many ways you are going to immediately use this knowledge to *make more money NOW*:

_____

_____

_____

_____

_____

Note: Exercises for this chapter can be found in Part II, Section A.

CHAPTER 10

Make *"World-Class Excellent"* Persuasion a Permanent Part of Your Prosperous Lifestyle

Benefits of this Chapter
Time-released Suggestions
Closing Mission Statement
Vade Mecum

BENEFITS OF THIS CHAPTER

- *How to give suggestions that will be followed by others in the future.*
- *How to ask for what you want in the right way.*
- *Specific tools you can use for the rest of your life.*
- *How to communicate to others who you are and why you're special.*
- *Formats to follow for every situation.*

TIME-RELEASED SUGGESTIONS

1. **Tangibles-** This technique enables you to make sure that once you secure a commitment or agreement from people, they won't back out later. Here's how it works:

   - Get a commitment to something.
   - Create an arbitrary situation in the future where they might not be as excited with their commitment as they are *NOW*.
   - Ask them what will cause them to keep their commitment anyway.

2. **Ideas-** You can also do this with any idea you want to impress upon someone.

   The way *this works* is to:

   - Give a suggestion that you want the person to carry out.
   - Identify in your mind a time in the future that you want to remind the person of this suggestion.
   - Tell the person that when the time in the future happens, they will automatically remember this suggestion.
   - Use the PPPL, PPL, PL, LL format to do this.

It's very important to do this regularly when you get a commitment or agreement. This will save you much heartache.

CLOSING

On this subject, I anticipate that you realize nothing's better than an *excellent presentation* to help you secure an agreement - whether you are on the podium before an audience pushing your cause, speaking in any situation, writing, negotiating, or selling products.

When you *use these skills powerfully* they will usually ask you what the next step is. **Their mind will be dependent upon you for their next thought!**

In addition, there are also times when you want to directly ask for the commitment to your position or cause, or for the deal. The following two strategies are especially helpful in a selling or business context.

Strategy 1

It goes like this. After you have completed your presentation and it's time to secure the agreement, ask:

"Is there anything else you need to know in order to go ahead?"

This is great, because in this case, no really means yes! Also, if they say yes, then you still are in there and can get to the bottom line. Either way, you haven't lost the deal.

Strategy 2

This strategy goes *like this.* Again, after you have completed your presentation and it's time to secure the agreement, do the following:

1. Reiterate why you are there. (**"We got together today because..."**)
2. Say, **"We decided to take care of** (to handle, to fix, to do something about their Criteria List)**"**

3. Say, **"I would like to** (enroll you, have you hire my firm, schedule our first meeting, and so on) **for all the obvious reasons.**

4. Ask, **"Is this what you'd *like to do?"***

That's all there is to it. Usually, people will ask you how they can get involved with whatever you're doing once you have presented what you do well enough.

VADE MECUM GUIDE

Vade mecum is a fancy Latin word that means "always take it with me." This vade mecum is meant to be used as your personal guide to further enhance your persuasive power in any situation. These tools have been specifically organized and structured so you will constantly have a path towards *increased success.* They are:

1. **Mission Statement-** This can express why you are on this planet, your reason for being, who you are. The answers to these questions can be the content of what you say to others. This is a way to communicate to your target audience or clients that you, your policy, or your program — your service or product — will benefit them, and why you are the best of all choices.

    This information lets the others know who you are and what you can do for them in specific relation to their needs. Of utmost importance are the answers to question 4. You need to communicate to the marketplace what **only** you can do for them that no one else can.

    A word of advice about question 4. You must come up with a credible and convincing answer. If there is no answer you better come up with one, think one up, make some changes, or get out of the way. There are already too many unsound concepts being pushed, and too many mediocre companies doing business.

NOTE: Remember *"world class excellence"* is the only standard!

2. **Presupposition Vocabulary-** Remember that the key to ***using presuppositions powerfully*** is to stick many of them — at least three — in the sentence before you say what you want them to do. One of the many ways you can immediately begin to use this vocabulary is to have the words laying out on the top of your desk when you are making a phone call.

   For personal meetings, you may find it helpful to glance at the presuppositions vocabulary and the sitform (below) before the meeting.

3. **Sitforms-** Situation formats can be used as outlines for how every persuasion encounter can flow. The ones provided for telephone inquiries and personal meetings can give you an idea of how to construct your own scripts to use in your own particular situation. The generic situation formats can be used as an outline to guide you in almost any situation you will encounter.

4. **Procedures and Requirements Form-** A simple form you can use to assist you in eliciting the information you need to give the other person—or the group you are persuading—so you can convince them to do what you want.

5. **Review Checklists; Grading and charting-** The 21-Day Program will clearly reveal just how valuable the grading and charting are. This step and step 6 below are truly the most important keys to making this System work; **it is the "difference that makes the difference" to** *make more money NOW.*

Depending on what you want to concentrate on, you can focus on the Rapport or Comprehensive Checklists to continually cause persuasion peak performance enhancement. We recommend starting on the Rapport Checklist and staying with it until you ***master it.*** Then move on to the Comprehensive Checklist. It is helpful to grade and chart either at day's end or — preferably — after each contact. What you do next is see what you scored lowest on; that one skill is what you will concentrate on enhancing during your next contact.

6. **Outcome Charts-** *NOW* that you realize the importance of grading and charting, we would like to add the concept of charting the outcomes you would like to realize, plus the outcomes you need to achieve along the way. For example, the **Macro Outcome Form** lists various indicators to chart. One such indicator is the amount of monthly income you want. In order to get that monthly income where you want it, there are steps along the way like sending mailings, making appointments, etc. On the **7-Step Tracking Form** you can keep track of each of your clients as they progress throughout the steps of your campaign. The **Micro Outcome Form** allows you to define the conversion rates of each step. For more detailed information about the design and application of these Systems, read our report, "Marketing Made Easy."

NOTE: Remember the key to *make more money NOW* is grading and charting.

Mission Statement

1. **What is my (our) true purpose? Who are our customers? Whom do we serve?**

   _____

   _____

   _____

   _____

2. **What is it that we contribute to add value to those we serve?**

   _____

   _____

   _____

   _____

3. What will be better for others as a result of dealing business with us? How does that relate to our customers' outcomes?

_____

_____

_____

_____

4. What is special about us? What can you do for me (the other person) that no one else can? Specifically, why should I do business with you out of all the possible companies in the marketplace?

_____

_____

_____

_____

5. What is our company vision of where we will be in one year? In ten years?

_____

_____

_____

_____

6. To what extent is this vision already shared on all levels of the company? To what degree does this vision compel all employees to continually strive for world class excellence? To what degree is your vision communicated to your clients so that they are compelled to share it too and cause you to achieve it?

_____

_____

_____

_____

Key Words to Keep With You for Enhancing Your Use of the Five Categories of Presuppositions

Adverb/Adjective

some	all	many	begin	easily	naturally
readily	infinitely	unlimited	continue	begin	still
already	repeatedly	usually	finally	most	truly

Awareness
(also include the gerund form [the "ing" as in realizing] for each word)

realize	aware	know	understand	think	feel
puzzle	speculate	perceive	discover	experience	accomplish
fulfill	grasp	reconsider	weigh	consider	assume
conceive	wonder				

Time/Number

before	former	current(ly)	while	was	during
after	when	continue	foremost	eventually	later
first(ly)	until	second(ly)	highest	early	other
chief	another	earliest	latest	more	*NOW*
since	immediately	in addition to			

Cause and Effect

kindles	causes	allows	forces	permits	determines
invokes	settles	proves	makes	stimulates	generates
because	stop	creates	verifies	causes	justifies
constitutes	brings to pass				

Spatial

against	along	among	apart from	around
aside from	behind	below	beneath	beyond
along with	down	from	above in	including
from behind	from under	without	in place of	off
out of	around	short of	through	under
uncover	off the top	underlying	touching	close(er)
near(er)	further	expanded	toward on	undergone
upward(ly)	dissect	cut away	lower	separate
withdraw(ing)		proceed(ed)(ing)		enlarge(d)(ing)

Situation- *Inquiry on the phone*

1. **Outcomes-** *Get very interested*
   Work with us
   Convince yourself
   Meet with me
   Make More Money NOW

2. **See, hear, feel and make sense of a movie with you easily and naturally achieving your goal, step into the movie.**

3. **Gain, calibrate and maintain rapport throughout.**

4. **Open, pace lead outcome directives. (PPPL, PPL, PL, LL).**

   "Your name is _____. You are calling me today about _____, Your qualifications are _____. And before you can discover how naturally you can *get very interested* about our company, you need to *meet with us personally...*

   ...So that you can *convince yourself* it's best to work with us to, foremost, *make more money NOW*. Would it be better for you to *come here* on _____ or _____?"

5. **Convincer Strategy-** *"How do (did) you make the decision to _____?"*

   "How many times do you need to _____ to convince yourself?"

6. **Criteria List-** *"What is important to you about _____?"*

   "How does that benefit you?"

7. **Cycle, Calibrate-** When you cycle through their strategy and Criteria List and get them right, let that correct cycle be the first PPP of your PPPL, PPL, PL, LL. Keep cycling through their strategy and Criteria List (linked with what you want them to do) repeatedly until you achieve your outcome.

8. Ask to *meet with me* for all the obvious reasons.

Situation- *Personal meeting*

1. **Outcomes-** *Establish rapport   Come to the seminar*
   Get very interested   Make more money NOW
   Convince yourself   Become successful NOW
   Work with us   Refer others

2. **See, hear, feel and make sense of a movie with you easily and naturally achieving your goal, step into the movie.**

3. **Gain, calibrate and maintain rapport throughout.**

4. **Open, pace lead outcome directives. (PPPL, PPL, PL, LL).**

   "You and I have _____ before, and as we _____ today, you may already discover how naturally you can ***get very interested***. Among the many obvious reasons to ***get very interested***. I am _____ you is that you can proceed immediately to truly ***convince yourself*** of some of the many reasons for you to make the decision to ***work with us***.

   One of the many benefits you receive when you ***work with us*** is that you will begin foremost to ***become more successful NOW***. Of course you may already grasp that this will allow you to continue to expand further to continue upwardly to repeatedly ***make more money NOW***."

   "Are you aware how important it is to ***refer others*** to our company?"

5. **Convincer Strategy-** *"How do (did) you make the decision to _____?"*
   *"How many times do you need to _____ to **convince yourself**?"*

6. **Criteria List-** *"What is important to you about _____?"*
   "How does that benefit you?"

7. **Cycle, Calibrate-** When you cycle through their strategy and Criteria List and get them right, let that correct cycle be the first PPP of your PPPL, PPL, PL, LL. Keep cycling through their strategy and Criteria List (linked with what you want them to do) repeatedly until you achieve your outcome.

8. Ask to *work with me* for all the obvious reasons.

Situation- *Generic*

1. *Determine your outcome* clearly.

2. **See, hear, feel and make sense of a movie with you easily and naturally achieving your goal, step into the movie.**

3. **Gain, calibrate and maintain rapport throughout.**

4. **Open pace lead outcome directives**. (PPPL, PPL, PL, LL).

5. **Convincer strategy-***"How do you know when _____?"*

*"How many times to **convince yourself?**"*

6. **Elicit Criteria List-***"What is important about _____?"*

"How does that benefit you?"

7. **Cycle, Calibrate-** When you cycle through their strategy and Criteria List and get them right, let that correct cycle be the first PPP of your PPPL, PPL, PL, LL. Keep cycling through their strategy and Criteria List (linked with what you want them to do) repeatedly until you achieve your outcome.

8. Ask to *work together* for all the obvious reasons.

Procedures and requirements form

Name _____ Code _____

Phone _____

Fax _____ Email _____

Qualifications

_____

_____

_____

_____

Procedural Requirements

What	Number of times	V, A, K, CL (Is it something visual, auditory, kinesthetic, or Criteria List?)

Criteria List Requirements

_____

_____

_____

Benefits- Toward/Away

_____

_____

Rapport Review Checklist

Review the previous encounter from the third person perspective, i.e. as if you are <u>watching yourself</u> on a movie screen. Circle the number which best represents your experience: 1 being not at all; 5 being fully.

How strongly did you:

1. Clearly determine your outcome?   **1 2 3 4 5**

2. Visualize a complete success movie, step into it?   **1 2 3 4 5**

3. Mirror the breath?   **1 2 3 4 5**

4. Mirror the voice tone, tempo, rhythm?   **1 2 3 4 5**

5. Mirror the posture?   **1 2 3 4 5**

NOW, **review again from the** *first person perspective* **(as if you are <u>in</u> the movie) and** *be seeing, hearing, feeling and making sense of, doing it perfectly.* **Then, looking back** *NOW*, **having already made so many changes, what are some of the many things will you have already been doing differently? I will already have been...**

Comprehensive Review Checklist

Review the previous encounter from the third person perspective, i.e. as if you are <u>watching yourself</u> on a movie screen. Circle the number which best represents your experience: 1 being not at all; 5 being fully.

How strongly did you:

1. Clearly determine your outcome?   1 2 3 4 5

2. Visualize a complete success movie, step into it?   1 2 3 4 5

3. Gain initial rapport?   1 2 3 4 5

4. Calibrate and maintain rapport throughout?   1 2 3 4 5

5. Use positive presuppositions?   1 2 3 4 5

6. Elicit strategy process, cycle, calibrate, mirror strategy

    using pace, lead, outcome directives to achieve outcome?   1 2 3 4 5

7. Elicit Criteria List, cycle, calibrate, mirror Criteria List   1 2 3 4 5

    using pace, lead, outcome directives to achieve outcome?

8. How effectively did you use pace lead language throughout?   1 2 3 4 5

9. How effectively did you use presuppositions throughout?   1 2 3 4 5

10. How effectively did you use hidden outcome   1 2 3 4 5

    directives throughout?

NOW, review again from the *first person perspective* (as if you are <u>in</u> the movie) and *be seeing, hearing, feeling and making sense of, doing it perfectly.* Then, looking back *NOW,* having already made so many changes, what are some of the many things will you have already been doing differently? I will already have been…

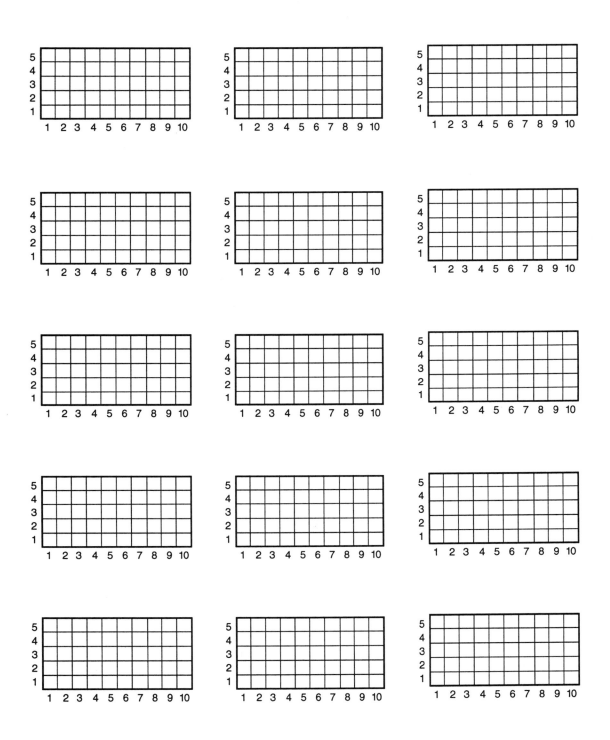

131

7-Step Tracking Form

Code_____   Step 1____   Step 2____   Step 3____   Step 4____

                              Step 5____   Step 6____   Step 7____

Code_____   Step 1____   Step 2____   Step 3____   Step 4____

                              Step 5____   Step 6____   Step 7____

Code_____   Step 1____   Step 2____   Step 3____   Step 4____

                              Step 5____   Step 6____   Step 7____

Code_____   Step 1____   Step 2____   Step 3____   Step 4____

                              Step 5____   Step 6____   Step 7____

Code_____   Step 1____   Step 2____   Step 3____   Step 4____

                              Step 5____   Step 6____   Step 7____

Code_____   Step 1____   Step 2____   Step 3____   Step 4____

                              Step 5____   Step 6____   Step 7____

Macro Outcome Form

1. **Monthly earning.**

2. **Total savings amount.**

3. **Total earnings this year.**

4. **Average size earning per client.**

5. **Production vs. capital expenditure on marketing.**

6. **Number of pieces sent per week.**

7. **Number of inquiries per week.**

8. **Number of outgoing calls per week.**

9. **Number of appointments made per week.**

10. **Number of people seen per week.**

11. **Percentage of appointments kept per week.**

12. **Conversion ratio.**

13. **Number of new accounts per month.**

14. **Total number of active accounts.**

Micro Outcome Form

Step 1 Gross number _____

  % Conversion _____

Step 2 Gross number _____

  % Conversion _____

Step 3 Gross number _____

  % Conversion _____

Step 4 Gross number _____

  % Conversion _____

Step 5 Gross number _____

  % Conversion _____

Step 6 Gross Number _____

  % Conversion _____

Step 7 Gross Number _____

  % Conversion _____

PART II, SECTION A
THE 21-DAY PROGRAM:
AN 11-MINUTE PER DAY TRAINING REGIME

Here's how *it works*:

Each day you will have a major training focus. That will be the skill that you will exercise most during that days peak performance enhancement. On each days page will be how to do the exercise.

So you do the exercise that day. At the end of the day, or after every encounter, you review your peak performance enhancement with the review checklist process, which can be found in Chapter 10 in the Vade Mecum Guide. After reviewing your performance and discovering how to improve, you then chart your performance to make a visual record. Put the chart on the wall for frequent reference.

NOW comes the most important question of all. What is my **aha**? = How am I going to use what I have learned today to *make more money NOW*?

Next it's time for the reality check. Where have I come from, where am I *NOW*, and where am I going in relation to *making more money NOW*?

To make sure that your 21-Day Program is all inclusive and powerful we have given you a way to naturally *make more money NOW* even while you sleep! That is where the Night Tapes come into play.

In order to ensure you stay on track, motivated and in the right frame of mind, we have also included stimulating questions to generate within you the resources to continually *enhance your peak performance*.

1. **Today's training focus:** Experience has shown that we really *learn something well* by doing one thing over and over again until that one skill is learned so well through

conscious repetition that the behavior becomes natural.

You have the information, the facts of how *the System works* from reading the first part of this book. The real learning comes from the doing.

You will be given an exercise to focus on for the entire day. These exercises are graduated so that as you *gain proficiency*, you can always *add more* to keep the exercises challenging.

2. **Grading and Charting:** Charting and grading your peak performance enhancement can be done throughout the day after each meeting or phone call or at the end of the day. The Rapport and Comprehensive Checklists as well as the Macro and Micro Outcome Form charting are **the key** to *making more money NOW.* They are found in Chapter 10 in the Vade Mecum Guide. You have our permission to photocopy these Checklists and charts. Keep the charts up on a wall or in a prominent place where you can see them frequently. When you *chart on a daily basis* for the next 21 days, you will *make more money NOW.*

To grade yourself with the Rapport and Comprehensive Checklists, you first make a mental movie of your meeting or phone call. See the movie as if you are watching yourself on the movie screen. This we call the third person perspective.

You look objectively at your peak performance enhancement and grade it on how strongly you did the skill in question on a 1 to 5 scale, with 1 being not at all and 5 being fully.

This is the stage where you objectively critique your peak performance enhancement and examine where and how you can make the necessary modifications.

For example, you are asked to review on the movie how strongly you determined your outcome. If you had determined no outcome whatsoever, you would put 1 and if you fully determined and experienced the outcome you would give yourself a 5.

NOW that you have circled the grades which you gave yourself on the review checklist skills, it's time to chart your peak performance enhancement. What you do is put an x on the corresponding number on the chart. This allows you to begin to see the pattern of your continual peak performance enhancement.

You will note there is room on each chart for ten encounters (persuasion opportunities) or ten days. What you can do is to chart your peak performance enhancement ten days at a time or ten encounters at a time. You can also tape a continuance of the chart on the wall. Do whatever works for you! However, you <u>must</u> chart to truly *make more money*.

NOW you are ready to finish the review checklist step by reviewing your peak performance enhancement from the first person perspective, as if you are actually the actor in the movie. In this process you are seeing, hearing feeling and making sense of performing with absolute perfection and elegance.

Next you answer this question- Looking back *NOW*, having already made so many changes, what are some of the many things I will have already been doing differently? I will already have been…(write or say what you will have already been doing differently.)

NOTE: Since you will graduate in your peak performance enhancement, we will recommend which skills to review and chart as you go along with the 21-Day Program so you can increase your ability.

3. **Aha:** You have exercised and reviewed your peak performance enhancement. *NOW* is the time to answer the question: "How am I going to use what I have just learned to *make more money NOW*?"

    This is the time to think of all the many ways you are going to use that day's skill, and how to integrate that learning into your repertoire to *make more money NOW*.

4. **Reality check:** This is where you review nightly where you have improved and where you are going in relation to *making more money NOW*. The Reality Check is found in Part II, Section C.

5. **Night tapes:** The night tapes have multifold purposes. One is to have something for your mind to listen to over and over to get a certain message across. The main message is for you to *make more money NOW*. The tapes have all been written using the patterns you are learning so that when you *make the tapes* you are practicing the patterns. When you hear your own voice, it will *reinforce the patterns* in your mind as well. The night tape scripts are found in Part II, Section B.

6. **Daily questions:** These questions assist you in developing the right mental attitude to *make more money NOW*. Quality answers cause a quality life. The questions are found in Part II, Section D.

DAY 1

1. **Today's training focus: Persuasion Peak Performance Enhancement**

   Exercise 1: New Outcome Generation.

      Perform the following procedure beforehand with everyone you meet:

   A) Determine the outcome you want from each contact. Ask yourself, "After I have already achieved my new goal, what will I look like?"
      (Put your eyes and head down and to the <u>left</u>.)

   B) Picture yourself achieving your goal as if you are watching yourself in a movie.
      (Look up and to the <u>right</u>.)

   C) Step into the picture so you feel yourself doing what you pictured.
      (Put your eyes and head down and to the <u>right</u>.)

   D) Compare these feelings to feelings from a similar past success.
      (Keep your eyes and head turned down and to the <u>right</u>.)

   E) When it feels the same, you can proceed to seize the new goal. If it does not feel the same yet, find what's missing and add it to your outcome. Then redo the process until it feels the same as the similar past success.

   NOTE: Some of you will have to turn your head to the opposite side indicated above.

   For example, right, left, left, left.

2. **Persuasion Peak Performance Rapport Review Checklist:**

   Grading and Charting.

3. **Aha: How am I going to use what I have learned today to *make more money NOW*?**

4. **Reality Check.**

5. **Night tapes.**

6. **Daily Questions.**

DAY 2

1. **Today's training focus: Persuasion Peak Performance Enhancement Exercise 2: Mirroring the breath.**

   Throughout every contact mirror the breath of each person you come in contact with. Once you are fully mirroring the breath, cause yourself to have a feeling of extreme desire and excitement.

2. **Persuasion Peak Performance Enhancement Rapport Review Checklist: Grading and Charting.**

3. **Aha: How am I going to use what I have learned today to *make more money NOW*?**

4. **Reality Check.**

5. **Night tapes.**

6. **Daily Questions.**

DAY 3

1. **Today's training focus: Persuasion Peak Performance Enhancement**

    Exercise 3: Bonding with the eyes.

    Throughout every contact mirror the breath of each person you come in contact with.

    Next, whenever you make eye appropriate eye contact, imagine that you are pushing energy which exits from your right eye into the other person's eye opposite (their left eye). At the same time pull energy with your left eye out of the other person's eye opposite (their right eye).

2. **Persuasion Peak Performance Enhancement Rapport Review Checklist: Grading and Charting.**

3. **Aha: How am I going to use what I have learned today to *make more money NOW*?**

4. **Reality Check.**

5. **Night tapes.**

6. **Daily Questions.**

DAY 4

1. **Today's training focus: Persuasion Peak Performance Enhancement**

   Exercise 4: Bonding with the eyes.

   Throughout every contact mirror the breath of each person.

   Next, whenever you make appropriate eye contact, imagine you are pushing energy that exits from your right eye into the other person's eye opposite (their left eye). At the same time pull energy with your left eye out of the other person's eye opposite (their right eye).

   We add on to yesterday's exercise: Imagine and visualize a continuous stream of energy streaming out of your right eye into their left eye and streaming out of their right eye pulling into your left eye. Imagine this flow as a luminous white light of energy and *NOW* notice what happens.

2. **Persuasion Peak Performance Enhancement Rapport Review Checklist: Grading and Charting.**

3. **Aha: How am I going to use what I have learned today to *make more money NOW*?**

4. **Reality Check.**

5. **Night tapes.**

6. **Daily Questions.**

DAY 5

1. **Today's training focus: Persuasion Peak Performance Enhancement**

   Exercise 5: Bonding with the eyes.

   Throughout each contact mirror the breath of every person you come in contact with. Next, whenever you make eye appropriate eye contact, imagine that you are pushing energy which exits from your right eye into the other person's eye opposite (their left eye). At the same time pull energy with your left eye out of the other person's eye opposite (their right eye). Imagine and visualize a continuous stream of energy streaming out of your right eye into their left eye and streaming out of their right eye pulling into your left eye. Imagine this flow as a luminous white light of energy and *NOW* notice what happens.

   We add on to yesterday's exercise: *NOW* simultaneously, inhale and imagine a luminous white light of energy expanding from your center and see (visualize) that energy enveloping the other person. *NOW* exhale and bring that energy back into your center and up your spinal column through the brain and out.

2. **Persuasion Peak Performance Enhancement Rapport Review Checklist: Grading and Charting.**

3. **Aha: How am I going to use what I have learned today to** *make more money NOW*?

4. **Reality Check.**

5. **Night tapes.**

6. **Daily Questions.**

DAY 6

1. **Today's training focus: Persuasion Peak Performance Enhancement**

    Exercise 6: Mirroring the voice.

    Today, with everyone you come in contact with, mirror the tempo and rhythm of their voice. Speak at the speed and rate they do.

2. **Persuasion Peak Performance Enhancement Rapport Review Checklist: Grading and Charting.**

3. **Aha: How am I going to use what I have learned today to *make more money NOW*?**

4. **Reality Check.**

5. **Night tapes.**

6. **Daily Questions.**

DAY 7

1. **Today's training focus: Persuasion Peak Performance Enhancement**

   Exercise 7: Mirroring the posture.

   Today you will mirror the posture of everyone you come in contact with.

2. **Persuasion Peak Performance Enhancement Rapport Review Checklist: Grading and Charting.**

3. **Aha: How am I going to use what I have learned today to *make more money NOW*?**

4. **Reality Check.**

5. **Night tapes.**

6. **Daily Questions.**

DAY 8

1. **Today's training focus: Persuasion Peak Performance Enhancement**

   Exercise 8: Pacing and leading with the breath.

   Today, with everyone you come in contact with, begin by pacing your breath (i.e. mirroring the other person's inhalations and exhalations) with the other person's breathing. Next pace your rate of speech to the other person's breathing and finally tap your finger, hand or foot to that rate.

   When rapport has been established in your opinion you begin to lead with the breath while you steer the conversation in the direction of your outcome.

2. **Persuasion Peak Performance Enhancement Rapport Review Checklist: Grading and Charting.**

3. **Aha: How am I going to use what I have learned today to *make more money NOW*?**

4. **Reality Check.**

5. **Night tapes.**

6. **Daily Questions.**

DAY 9

1. **Today's training focus: Persuasion Peak Performance Enhancement**

   Exercise 9: Comprehensive Pacing.

   With each person you come into contact with today, appropriately mirror all the other person's behaviors: their posture, rate of breathing, speech, the verbal predicates they use as well as match to their eye accessing cues.

   Do what the other person does allowing a lag-time of 3-4 counts. Be aware of muscle tension, overall minute details.

2. **Persuasion Peak Performance Enhancement Rapport Review Checklist: Grading and Charting.**

3. **Aha: How am I going to use what I have learned today to** *make more money NOW*?

4. **Reality Check.**

5. **Night tapes.**

6. **Daily Questions.**

DAY 10

1. **Today's training focus: Persuasion Peak Performance Enhancement**

    Exercise 10: Pacing and Leading.

    Begin every contact by mirroring all that is possible. Start out with a lag-time of three beats. Gradually reduce lag-time and eventually go to no lag-time. Then change the subject and lead in the direction of your outcome.

2. **Persuasion Peak Performance Enhancement Rapport Review Checklist: Grading and Charting.**

3. **Aha: How am I going to use what I have learned today to *make more money NOW*?**

4. **Reality Check.**

5. **Night tapes.**

6. **Daily Questions.**

DAY 11

1. **Today's training focus: Persuasion Peak Performance Enhancement**

   Exercise 11: Decision strategy elicitation and utilization.

   Ask everyone you come into contact with, "How did/do you decide to X?"

   Elicit the strategy, cycle through to be sure you have it. Then let that correct cycle be your first PPL using everything, that is, PPPL, PPL, PL, LL, presuppositions, and hidden outcome directives, etc., all packed in together to persuade the person to do what you want.

2. **Persuasion Peak Performance Enhancement Comprehensive Review Checklist: Grading and Charting.**

3. **Aha: How am I going to use what I have learned today to *make more money NOW*?**

4. **Reality Check.**

5. **Night tapes.**

6. **Daily Questions.**

DAY 12

1. **Today's training focus: Persuasion Peak Performance Enhancement**

   Exercise 12: Motivation strategy elicitation and utilization.

   Ask everyone you come into contact with : "How did/do you motivate yourself to X?" Elicit the strategy, cycle through to be sure you have it. Then let that correct cycle be your first PPL using everything, that is, PPPL, PPL, PL, LL, presuppositions, and hidden outcome directives, etc., all packed in together to persuade the person to do what you want.

2. **Persuasion Peak Performance Enhancement Comprehensive Review Checklist: Grading and Charting.**

3. **Aha: How am I going to use what I have learned today to *make more money NOW*?**

4. **Reality Check.**

5. **Night tapes.**

6. **Daily Questions.**

DAY 13

1. **Today's training focus: Persuasion Peak Performance Enhancement**

    Exercise 13: Excellence in strategy elicitation and utilization.

    Ask everyone you come into contact with, "How did/do you do what you are excellent at?" Repeat it back right to make sure you have it. *NOW* you can use their strategy to train yourself to be excellent at that particular skill.

2. **Persuasion Peak Performance Enhancement Comprehensive Review Checklist: Grading and Charting.**

3. **Aha: How am I going to use what I have learned today to *make more money NOW*?**

4. **Reality Check.**

5. **Night tapes.**

6. **Daily Questions.**

DAY 14

1. **Today's training focus: Persuasion Peak Performance Enhancement**

   Exercise 14: Convincer strategy elicitation and utilization.

   Elicit convincer strategies from everyone you come in contact with. Ask, "How do you know when you have found an X (fill in the context) that you will Y (fill in the context)*?* Then ask, "How many times to *convince yourself?*" Elicit the strategy, cycle through to be sure you have it. Then let that correct cycle be your first PPL using everything, that is, PPPL, PPL, PL, LL, presuppositions, and hidden outcome directives, etc., all packed in together to persuade the person to do what you want.

2. **Persuasion Peak Performance Enhancement Comprehensive Review Checklist: Grading and Charting.**

3. **Aha: How am I going to use what I have learned today to *make more money NOW*?**

4. **Reality Check.**

5. **Night tapes.**

6. **Daily Questions.**

DAY 15

1. **Today's training focus: Persuasion Peak Performance Enhancement**

   Exercise 15: Instant decision to agree (buy).

   Do this with everyone you come in contact with. Make deep rapport.

   Calibrate, and observe closely. Ask, "When have you looked at something and you immediately knew it was absolutely right for you. It was the perfect thing for you, and you have always felt right about that decision or purchase since you made it?" Hint: You might need to ask, "What was it?" Notice and remember exactly where they focus their eyes in space (in the "good convincer" spot), right before they say yes or nod their head. Change the subject, and deepen rapport. Present your contract, what you want them to do, etc., in the exact spot they focused their eyes in response to the previous question, and persuade them to do what you want.

   Peak Performance Enhancement Comprehensive Review Checklist: Grading and Charting.

3. **Aha: How am I going to use what I have learned today to *make more money NOW*?**

4. **Reality Check.**

5. **Night tapes.**

6. **Daily Questions.**

DAY 16

1. **Today's training focus: Persuasion Peak Performance Enhancement**

   Exercise 16: Inducing and anchoring agreement.

   Do this with everyone you meet. Make deep rapport. Calibrate and observe closely. Ask, "When have you looked at something and you immediately knew it was absolutely right for you. It was the perfect thing for you, and you have always felt right about that decision or purchase since you made it?" Hint: You might need to ask, "What was it?"

   We add on to yesterday's exercise: Right as they say yes or nod their head, touch them in a subtle, non-provocative way. If you are not in a position or a situation where you can touch the person, make a specific gesture with your hand downward. Over the phone, click your pen into the mouthpiece. Change the subject, and deepen rapport. Talk about what you want them to do. Calibrate.

   Present your contract, what you want them to do, etc. and touch them (or make the same gesture or sound exactly as before, and persuade them to do what you want.

2. **Persuasion Peak Performance Enhancement Comprehensive Review Checklist: Grading and Charting.**

3. **Aha: How am I going to use what I have learned today to *make more money NOW*?**

4. **Reality Check.**

5. **Night tapes.**

6. **Daily Questions.**

DAY 17

1. **Today's training focus: Persuasion Peak Performance Enhancement**

   Exercise 17: Inducing and anchoring agreement.

   This time ask the same question as yesterday. As you do so, notice where they focus their eyes as well as making a touch, gesture, or sound. Then present what you want them to do. Present it in the "good convincer" spot, make the gesture or sound again, and persuade them to do what you want.

2. **Persuasion Peak Performance Enhancement Comprehensive Review Checklist: Grading and Charting.**

3. **Aha: How am I going to use what I have learned today to *make more money NOW*?**

4. **Reality Check.**

5. **Night tapes.**

6. **Daily Questions.**

DAY 18

1. **Today's training focus: Persuasion Peak Performance Enhancement Exercise 18: Criteria List elicitation and utilization.**

   Elicit the Criteria List of every one you come into contact with by asking, "What is important about...?" Elicit the Criteria List, cycle through to be sure you have it. Then let that correct cycle be your first PPL using everything, i.e. PPPL, PPL, PL, LL, pre-suppositions, and hidden outcome directives, etc., all packed in together to persuade the person to do what you want.

2. **Persuasion Peak Performance Enhancement Comprehensive Review Checklist: Grading and Charting.**

3. **Aha: How am I going to use what I have learned today to *make more money NOW*?**

4. **Reality Check.**

5. **Night tapes.**

6. **Daily Questions.**

DAY 19

1. **Today's training focus: Persuasion Peak Performance Enhancement**

   Exercise 19: PPPL speak.

   With everyone you come in contact with, use the "look of confusion." That is to say, look through them as if you are focusing about two feet behind the back of their head. Also: speak with PPP-L, PP-L, P-L, LL pattern with every person you come into contact with to get them to do what you want.

2. **Persuasion Peak Performance Enhancement Comprehensive Review Checklist: Grading and Charting.**

3. **Aha: How am I going to use what I have learned today** *make more money NOW*?

4. **Reality Check.**

5. **Night tapes.**

6. **Daily Questions.**

DAY 20

1. **Today's training focus: Persuasion Peak Performance Enhancement**

   Exercise 20: Presuppositions.

   Utilize the presupposition vocabulary with everyone you come in contact with to get them to do what you want. Discover how easy it is to use more than 3 presupposition words per sentence.

2. **Persuasion Peak Performance Enhancement Comprehensive Review Checklist: Grading and Charting.**

3. **Aha: How am I going to use what I have learned today to** *make more money NOW*?

4. **Reality Check.**

5. **Night tapes.**

6. **Daily Questions.**

DAY 21

1. **Today's training focus: Persuasion Peak Performance Enhancement**

   Exercise 21: Hidden outcome directives.

   Mark off hidden outcome directives, three per sentence, with every person you come into contact with to get them to do what you want.

2. **Persuasion Peak Performance Enhancement Comprehensive Review Checklist: Grading and Charting.**

3. **Aha: How am I going to use what I have learned today to *make more money NOW*?**

4. **Reality Check.**

5. **Night tapes.**

6. **Daily Questions.**

PART II, SECTION B
NIGHT TAPE SCRIPTS
NIGHT TAPE SCRIPT GUIDE

The night tapes deliver multiple benefits. One is to have something for your mind to listen to over and over to get a certain message across. The tapes have all been written using the patterns you are learning so that when you make the tapes you are practicing the patterns and when you hear your own voice it will reinforce the patterns in your mind as well.

For Tapes A, D, E and F, use a 120-minute tape and keep reading the script over and over until you record on both sides.

For Tapes B and C, use a three-minute endless loop tape like old answering machines use and just read the script once.

Whenever you encounter a "P" when recording the tapes, put in your own pacing statements.

Whenever you encounter an "L," which symbolizes "Lead," put in your own leading statements, that is, what you want to achieve.

When you encounter a blank, shown as _____, put in what you desire or want.

At night, listen to these tapes before you got to sleep. You'll find they will cause you to fall into a refreshing sleep. Turn the volume down just enough to hear it but not loud enough to disturb you.

When you make the tapes, use it as a way to practice and get feedback on your rhythm of speech and delivery of hidden outcome directives.

How to read the scripts:

1. The first time you record, focus on talking at a rate of about 1 beat per second and pause between each and every word.

2. *NOW* we start to turn up your ability to deliver the hidden outcome directives. You will notice that there are some phrases that are in ***bold and italic***. They are the hidden outcome directives. This time when you record, maintain the beat of about one per second. Pause for a count of 12 before and after you say the hidden outcome directive.

3. *NOW* whenever you come to the hidden outcome directives while recording, increase or decrease your tone of voice significantly.

4. This time, whenever you come to a hidden outcome directive, either say it very loud or almost in a whisper.

5. This time do all three: pause for 12 beats before and after, change your tone, change the volume of your voice—all at the same time.

The key to 2-5 is to really exaggerate your delivery

You'll be amazed at the power of this to:

A) Improve your ability to ***give hidden outcome directives***.

B) Cause you to ***naturally*** talk in this pattern—without even thinking about them.

C) Cause you to ***make more money NOW!***

Night Tape A

While you look at a spot in front of you as you hear me talking with you and as feel yourself lay there and you see yourself *listen closely* that causes your unconscious mind to immediately feel you can *realize completely* to see that your unconscious mind will above all hear and feel immediately to *become more successful NOW*. And as you see yourself *relax completely* you hear your unconscious mind begin immediately to *become aware* that your continual feeling of success will truly see itself *expand farther* and among the many benefits is that you hear as your unconscious mind is able to feel itself *become aware NOW* that this message has already seen itself started to *penetrate deeply* to hear your unconscious at its deepest core. The more I feel the experience that the message is able to hear itself *penetrate deeply* the more powerful it will feel itself *take effect immediately* into my deepest core and the more naturally and easily I see it *become aware* that I hear it immediately *feel good* because I see that I know that I will easily and naturally hear it as I feel myself *make more money NOW*. And I see myself expand beyond that to hear myself *feel happy*. See and hear yourself. *Feel very happy right NOW*. And as I view it effortlessly and easily hear myself think of the many ways to feel myself *become more successful NOW,* I will easily and naturally see myself *make more money NOW*. And as I hear myself *become more successful NOW,* I will begin immediately to *experience the feeling* of seeing myself easily and naturally expanding beyond that to hear and feel wonderful when I currently already begin immediately to *make more money NOW* I see that I will *make more money NOW* so that I do not have hear to worry about bills and can see myself enjoying, hearing, and feeling the *unlimited freedom* I desire. As the days go on I will easily and naturally see and hear myself *feel very confident* and I will easily and naturally see myself *become very successful* and the more I am able to hear myself *feel successful* the more I see that I tell you that you are already and immediately able to feel that you can *become successful NOW* as I see that I already begin immediately to hear and feel myself *make more money NOW*. As the days go on I see that I discover that I always immediately easily and naturally see, hear and feel myself *determine outcome strongly* and keep it in mind always and that I always easily and effortlessly see hear and feel myself *experience success NOW* in my imagination beforehand. As I see that I listen to this I can feel myself *experience unlimited success NOW* and see, hear and feel myself experience what I am seeing hearing and feeling successfully and see them in front of me and easily and naturally hear that *I feel very successful*. When I see and talk with everybody I immediately feel I easily and naturally always *use positive suppositions powerfully* I see hear and feel I always immediately *gain initial rapport* and effortlessly maintain it throughout so much so that I see hear and feel the person always is right there with me and easily and naturally immediately *loves me completely*. I see that I know that I always *use hidden outcome directives* I hear how I easily and naturally *use them powerfully* because I grasp that I easily and naturally so much so that I see they immediately *do what I say*. I feel wonderful as I effortlessly *elicit the Criteria List* in every contact that I always flawlessly *mirror back* to hear that I immediately easily and naturally feel wonderful as I *achieve my outcome*. I see that I will effortlessly *use all the skills* which I know are so powerful. I hear and feel that I always immediately *get what I want* and I am effortlessly able to see myself *make a lot of money* and will truly *make more money NOW* and I can hear myself *experience success in my bones* and can see myself laugh as I feel immediately as I see myself laugh as I *feel very good* as I *see the money*, laugh as I *experience joy* as I begin immediately to *truly see the money*, continually *hear the money*, and I *feel the money* in my hot little hands. *NOW* I already currently *see the green dollars*, while *NOW* I continually *hear the green dollars* and expand further to repeatedly *feel the green dollars*, and *NOW* I readily begin immediately to *see the bank balance growing* and I separately enlarge higher to *hear my bank balances growing* and *NOW* I see that I have unlimited wealth I hear myself *feel wonderful* because I effortlessly *make more money NOW* and in a few minutes I will go into a *very deep sleep* and during my sleep I will naturally and easily dream of the many ways that I will see, hear and feel the experience of success and I will expand beyond as my unconscious easily and naturally immediately is able to *help me powerfully* in my dreams in all the many ways that I will easily and naturally see myself *become very successful* and then I will hear immediately and infinitely wonderful feelings as I *become more successful NOW*. I will effortlessly *sleep well* so much so that upon rising I will easily and naturally *rest completely*, and upon waking I will see myself discovering and laughing as I feel myself experience boundless enthusiasm which will easily and naturally allow me to *experience complete success.* Sleep well, and *heal completely*.

Night Tape B

Seeing what your vision shows while you listen to the words I am saying as you feel your breathe cool in and warm out you allows you to begin immediately to easily and naturally continually and repeatedly experience yourself to *relax completely.* And as you view inside clearly to *completely relax* while you *listen closely* to the sound of your own thoughts that cause you to foremost underneath further currently repeatedly L and while you catch sharply PL that make you already truly underneath you infinitely see, hear and feel L.

Night Tape C

Seeing what your vision shows while you listen to the words I am saying as you feel your breathe cool in and warm out allows you to begin immediately to easily and naturally continually and repeatedly experiencing, you *relax completely*. And as you view inside clearly

PL while you *listen closely* to the sound of your own thoughts as you feel your breath further causes you to further currently LL. And as you PL while you L that immediately makes you continue to truly easily and naturally foremost see, hear and feel yourself LLL so as you PL this obviously already forces you to already easily and naturally continually and repeatedly immediately proceed to further LLLL.

Night Tape D

While you look at a spot in front of you as you hear me talking with you and as you feel yourself there and you see yourself *listen closely* that continues to cause your unconscious mind to truly immediately feel that while you can *realize completely* to see that your unconscious mind will while above all hear and feel immediately to infinitely *become more successful NOW*, (Put your name here.) And while as you continue to see yourself while you (Insert your name), might not have already noticed yourself *relaxing completely*, you continually hear your unconscious mind begin immediately to *become aware NOW* (Insert your name), that your continual feeling of success will truly see itself continually (Name). *expand farther* and among the many benefits is that you continue to hear is as your unconscious mind is able to feel itself *become aware NOW* (Name), that while this message has already seen itself continually and repeatedly started to *penetrate deeply* on many levels to hear your unconscious at its deepest core. The more I (Name) can feel the understanding experience that the message has already heard itself *penetrate deeply NOW* the more powerful it while continually will feel itself actually to *take effect immediately NOW* (Name), into my deepest core and the more naturally and easily continue to, (Name) immediately I see it *become aware* that I hear it immediately (Name) *feel good* (Name) because I see that I know that I will easily and naturally hear it as I feel myself *make more money NOW.* And I obviously see myself expand beyond that to hear myself, truly don't *feel too happy* too soon, wait for your next breath as you can see and hear yourself, (Name) *feel very happy right NOW*, (Name) and while I have already viewed it effortlessly and easily hear myself think of the many ways to feel myself already continue in many unlimited ways to *become more successful NOW*, (Name) so much more, (Name). I have already easily and quite naturally seen myself *make more money NOW.* And as I hear myself even *become more successful* than that I will already have begun immediately to continue to *experience the feeling* of seeing myself easily and naturally expanding beyond that to having heard and felt wonderful when I currently already beginning immediately, immediately beginning *NOW. NOW*, let me ask you, (Name) how would it feel if you knew starting right *NOW* that you already were well on your way to achieving all of your ultimate dreams including, of course, (fill in your desires here).

NOW, (Name) What would it feel like?

Do you believe it's possible? Where in the space in front of you is that belief located? Front, middle, down, right left, center? How does that belief sound, where is the sound coming from? How does that feel, and where is that feeling located?

NOW, (Name) let me ask you, do you believe that the sun is coming up tomorrow?

Where is that belief located?

Is it located at a different place than the belief that it is possible for you to achieve all of your ultimate dreams?

Does it sound different? Is the sound located at a different place than the belief that it's possible for you to achieve all of your ultimate dreams?

Does it feel different? Is the feeling located at a different place than this belief that it's possible for you to achieve all of your ultimate dreams?

If it does, move the belief that you will achieve all of your dreams to where the belief of the sun is located. Change the sound and the location of the sound. Change the feeling and continually change until you have them all located exactly where your belief that the sun will rise tomorrow is located. You may want to choose (Name). to actively design your future to achieve whatever it is that you desire. As the days go on I will easily and naturally see and hear myself *feel very confident* and I will easily and naturally see myself infinitely **become more successful NOW,** and moreover I, (Name), am able to hear myself successfully *feel more successful* the more I, (Name), see that I tell you that you are already and immediately have already felt able to feel that you can even **become more successful NOW**, (Name), as I see that I already begin immediately to hear and feel (Name) **make more money NOW**. As the days go on I see that I discover that I always immediately easily and naturally see, hear and feel myself **determine outcome strongly** and keep it in mind always and that I always easily and effortlessly see hear and feel myself *experience success NOW* in my imagination beforehand. As I see that I listen to this I can continually feel myself have, (Name), and **experience unlimited success NOW,** (Name), and successfully successful continually see, hear and feel myself successfully experience what I am seeing hearing and feeling successfully and see them in front of me and easily and naturally hear that moreover while I *feel more successful*. When I see and talk with everybody I immediately feel I easily and naturally always, (Name), use **positive suppositions powerfully**. While I, (Name), continue to see, hear and feel I always immediately **gain initial rapport** and quite effortlessly maintain it throughout so much so that I see hear and feel the person always is right there with me and easily and naturally immediately *love me completely*. I see that I know that I always *use **hidden outcome directives*** I hear how I easily and naturally **use them powerfully** because I grasp that I easily and naturally **use them right** so much so that I see they immediately **do what I say**. I feel wonderful as I effortlessly **elicit the Criteria List** emotions in every contact that I have, I shall always see that I always flawlessly **mirror it back** to hear that I immediately easily and naturally feel wonderful as I *achieve my outcome.* I see that I will effortlessly *use all the skills* which I know are so powerful. I hear and feel that I always immediately *get what I want* and I am effortlessly able to see myself *make a lot of money* and will truly *make more money NOW* and I can hear myself *experience success in my bones* and can see myself laugh as I feel immediately as I see myself laugh as **I** *feel very good* as I *see the money,* and laugh as I *experience joy* as I begin immediately to truly *see the money,* continually *hear the money,* and as I *feel the money* in my hot little hands. *NOW* I already currently *see the money, while NOW* I continually *hear the money* and expand further to repeatedly *feel the money* and *NOW* I readily begin immediately to *see the bank balance growing* and I separately enlarge higher to *hear the bank balances growing* and *NOW* I see that I have unlimited wealth I hear myself *feel wonderful* because I effortlessly *make more money NOW* and in a few minutes I will have already gone into a *very deep sleep NOW* and during my *sleep NOW* while I will naturally and easily dream of the many ways that I will continue to see, hear and feel the experience I desire and I will expand beyond as my unconscious easily and naturally immediately is able to *help me powerfully* in my dreams all the many ways that I will easily and naturally see myself *become more successful* and then I will hear immediately and infinitely wonderful feelings as I *become more successful NOW* will effortlessly *sleep well* so much so that upon rising I will easily and naturally *rest completely* and have upon waking I will see myself discover and laugh as I feel myself experience boundless enthusiasm which will easily and naturally allow me to *experience complete success.* Sleep well and *heal completely.*

Night Tape E

Before you observe the atmosphere around you while you continue to proceed to look at a spot in front of your eyes while you continually proceed to view the enveloping environment around you while you progress to immediately *listen closely* that foremost allows your unconscious mind to straight-away subsequently overhear itself, (Name), ***relax completely NOW***, (Name). While you continue to listen to your unconscious mind and begin to feel your chest rise and fall after you notice your breathing that simply causes you to repeatedly supremely at last finally _____ as you finally discover to know that you are aware that you watch yourself repeatedly and infinitely truly finally (Name) ***become more successful NOW*** (Name) And as you continue to picture yourself as you (Name) truly (Name) ***become more successful NOW*** (Name) understand to perpetually overhear your subliminal mind to ***begin immediately*** to eavesdrop all the unlimited ways to skillfully and automatically already completely (Name) ***use this information*** (Name) while you can understand obviously to cause it to (Name) ***become aware*** (Name) that your instinctive mind (Name) will truly touch itself repeatedly upwardly as above all ***expand farther*** to uncover that underlying you (Name) you discover (Name) yourself (Name) continually and repeatedly seizing ***immediate success*** after primarily and perpetually you ***initiate instantly*** to already continue to ***perceive NOW*** (Name) that these many messages have already gone beyond themselves to principally indeed started to further uncovered behind and while beneath to continue to upwardly powerfully continue to ***penetrate deeply*** (Name) into its incalculable immeasurable essence. (Name) Obviously (Name) ***NOW*** you can observe that I am ***NOW*** (Name) speaking to you (Name) ***NOW*** and while you might not have noticed that while this causes a sensation that this System will have moreover powerfully and infinitely (Name) ***NOW take effect immediately NOW*** (Name). ***NOW*** while this causes as you visualize all the many countless paths while you beginning immediately to continue to _____ with the instant outcome that when you ***commencing immediately*** while you continue to constantly (Name) commence ***NOW*** to _____ you will discover yourself narrating to yourself all the many ways to conceive how to immediately chiefly further unremittingly ***become more successful NOW*** (Name) ***NOW*** underlying this as it will cause you to upwardly on top foremost uncover to ***feel excited NOW*** about all the numerous divers maneuvers you can then ***establish NOW*** while to discover to profitably _____ to limitlessly and repeatedly ***master this*** so that you_____ (Name) You may not have noticed you see something while you are currently listening to me and as you may have noticed you feel your weight being supported that permits you to continually finally at last envision yourself ***become aware NOW*** that beneath all that you uncover closer on top to continually and repeatedly immediately (Name) ***feel good NOW***. (Name) As you continue to visualize into your imagination while you easily and naturally overhear your thoughts which will continue to cause you to discover the sensation of being able to ***use this System*** to upwardly and repeatedly _____. And as I (Name) visualize my imagination while able to expand upward further beyond that to hear myself ***feel happy NOW***. Separately already observe inwardly closer and hear inside yourself, as you (Name) ***feel very happy right NOW*** (Name) And as I foremost ***view it effortlessly*** and easily know to hear myself think of the many ways to feel myself ***use this System*** as I repeatedly know that I will chiefly ***become more successful NOW***. I will continue to accomplish to ***begin immediately*** to currently expand upward behind to ***experience the feeling*** of seeing myself easily and naturally expanding beyond that to hear and further already before ***feel wonderful*** when I currently infinitely ***beginning immediately*** truly continue to repeatedly infinitely obviously _____ I see that I will_____ And as the days go on I will easily and naturally see and hear myself ***feel very confident*** and I will easily and naturally ___ myself _____ and the more I am able to ___ myself ***feel prosperous*** the more I see that I tell you that you are already and immediately able to feel that you can absolutely immediately ***become more suc-***

cessful NOW as I see that I already *institute immediately* to hear and feel myself_____. As the days go on I see that I discover that I always immediately easily and naturally see, hear and feel myself *determine outcome strongly* and keep it in mind always and that I always easily and effortlessly see hear and feel myself *experience success NOW* in my imagination beforehand. As I see that I listen to this I can feel myself have *experience unlimited success* and see, hear and feel myself experience what I am seeing hearing and feeling successfully and see them in front of me and easily and naturally hear that I *feel very successful*. When I see and talk with everybody I immediately feel I easily and naturally always use *positive presuppositions powerfully* I see hear and feel I always immediately *gain initial rapport* and effortlessly maintain it throughout so much so that I observe, hear and feel the person always is right there with me and easily and naturally immediately *loves me completely*. I envision that I know that I always *use hidden outcome directives.* I hear how I effortlessly and instinctively *use them powerfully* because I grasp that I easily and naturally *use them right* so much so that I observe they immediately *do what I say.* I feel wonderful as I effortlessly *elicit the Criteria List emotions* in every contact that see that I always flawlessly *mirror them back* to hear that I immediately easily and naturally feel wonderful as I *achieve my outcome* I see that I will effortlessly *use all the skills* which I know are so powerful. When you _____ you ____ and ____ that you already immediately *get what you want* and I am effortlessly able to ____ myself _____ and will continue to truly repeatedly _____ and I can ____ myself _____ and can ____ myself laugh as I ____ immediately as I ____ myself laugh as I *feel very good* as I_____ laugh as I *experience joy* as I begin immediately to truly _____ continually ____ the _____ and I_____. *NOW* I already currently _____, while *NOW* I continually _____ and expand further to repeatedly _____ and *NOW* I readily begin immediately to rapidly _____ and I separately enlarge higher to

_____ and *NOW* I see that I have unlimited wealth I hear myself

feel wonderful because I effortlessly _____ and in a few minutes I will go into

a *very deep sleep* and during my sleep I will naturally and easily dream of the many ways that

I will see, hear and feel the experience of success and I will expand beyond as my uncon-

scious easily and naturally immediately is able to *help me powerfully* in my dreams all the

many ways that I will gracefully and innately see myself *become very successful* and then I

will hear swiftly and infinitely wonderful feelings as I *become more successful NOW.* I will

effortlessly *sleep well* so much so that upon rising I will easily and naturally *rest completely*

and have upon waking I will see myself discover and laugh as I feel myself experience

boundless enthusiasm which will obviously cause me to profoundly *experience complete*

success. Right *NOW*, *sleep well.*

Night Tape F

NOW you get to devise your own scripts for tapes. You can use the PPPL templates or

start from scratch. There are a few points to bear in mind:

1. External to internal pattern—Begin with the focus on the outside world and then move
    the focus to the inside world or thoughts.

2. Overlap representations—When you are designing, play with sequencing the representa-
    tional part—make the words follow a pattern of see, hear, feel. Next try—feel , see , hear.
    Let you imagination be your guide.

3. Use this pattern and see what happens—PPPPL. PPPLL. PPLLL. PLLLL

4. You already know this one-PPPL. PPL. PL. LL

Make as many combinations as you like of the above and experiment from here.

PART II, SECTION C
NIGHTLY REALITY CHECK

"Think about today in terms of what we have been doing and look at the difference between when you started and how you are *NOW*."

- Where do you think you are going in relation to *making more money NOW*?

- What have you discovered about *making more money NOW* that has surprised you?

- What new *making more money NOW* horizons are opening?

- What are you learning about *making more money NOW*?

- What have you discovered about *making more money NOW* that's important?

- What was new and different about *making more money NOW*?

PART II, SECTION D
DAILY QUESTIONS

A) What have you learned the most from today that you can use to *make more money NOW*?

B) What has the most room for improvement in your ability *to make more money NOW*?

C) How have you improved the most today in your ability *to make more money NOW*?

D) What are you enjoying most in your life right *NOW*? What about that do you naturally enjoy? How does that make you feel?

E) What are you most excited about in your life right *NOW*? What about that makes you excited? How does that make you feel?

F) What are you truly self confident about in your life right *NOW*? What about that makes you naturally self confident? How does that make you feel?

G) What are you most grateful about in your life right *NOW*? What about that makes you grateful? How does that make you feel?

PART III, APPENDIX 1
How to Tell If Someone Is Lying

Our multi million dollar mistake: Have you ever had someone who lied to you and took advantage of you? Do you wish you had a way to keep it from happening again? We do! Many years ago we did business with some people who promised us certain remuneration for outcomes we would achieve for them. While doing business with them, we always had a funny feeling we could not pin down. Once we had achieved the agreed upon outcomes, they did not live up to their part of the agreement. We discovered later on that all along they had no intention of keeping their part of the bargain.

This mistake cost us a fortune in lost income. Had we only known a way then to tell that they were lying to us! We then researched and developed a System that we could use to determine when someone is lying and when someone is telling the truth. This System is below and we hope it saves you from others taking advantage of you in the future:

1. **Make Rapport -**The first step to tell when someone is lying is to "get on the same wavelength" as they are on. You mirror the person's breathing, body posture, and when you talk with them, mirror their voice and inflection, and speak at the rate they are breathing. For example, when they are inhaling, you inhale at the same time. How do you know when someone is inhaling or exhaling? When someone is talking, they are exhaling; when they stop talking to take a breath, they are inhaling. So when they are talking, you exhale with them, and when they stop to take a breath, you inhale as well.

   If they are not talking, how do you tell? Look at their shoulders and notice the rise and fall of their shoulders against whatever is behind them. Try looking straight at someone, and then at a 45 degree angle to see which is easier for you.

When you speak at the rate they are breathing, using the same tone of voice as they are, you will get a feeling whether they are telling the truth or not. Also, speaking this way will easily and naturally cause them to be **compelled to tell you the truth, and divulge things they would not normally do.**

2. **The "human lie detector"** -The next step involves visually measuring the same things a lie detecting machine does. Either ask the person questions you already know the answers to, or look at them when they say things you know are true. While this is happening, you need to take a mental picture of the following:

a) **Their skin color-** is it light or dark.

b) **Skin muscle tone-** it shiny or dull.

c) **Lower lip-** is it expanded (lines not visible) or contracted (lines visible).

d) **Breathing-** the location, speed, and is it shallow or deep.

e) **Eye pupil dilation-** are the person's eye pupils small or large.

Take a mental picture and note the above visual clues the person in front of you is giving you. *NOW* you know the visual clues the person gives when he/she is telling the truth.

NOW make a statement about the person you know isn't true. Take a mental picture and note the visual cues when the person reacts to untrue things of a personal nature.

Alternatively, if possible, get the person to make statements you know are false. Take a mental picture of the visual cues the person displays when he/she is lying.

NOW as the person speaks, you will be able to tell when they are telling the truth, and when they are saying things they know are false. Merely compare the visual cues they are *NOW* showing to those displayed when they were either lying or telling the truth, and you'll know. It's just that easy and simple.

PART III, APPENDIX 2
DONOVAN INTERNATIONAL

4524 Curry Ford Road, Suite 237, Orlando, FL 32812
Voice 1 (407) 420-2538; Fax 1 (407) 370-0530
Toll free 1 (888) MyAlvin
E-Mail: alvin@interlan-stc.es

Appearances, Licenses, *Make More Money NOW* Shows, Educational Materials

APPEARANCES

Alvin G. Donovan III is a dynamic, compelling, and highly experienced speaker who delivers his powerful performance in an entertaining way. His in-house seminars can bring the enormous benefits of this unique System to your people. Or **book him** for an appearance at one of your events by calling 1-407-420-2538.

LICENSES

Are you eager to cash in on the enormous demand for public speakers? Launch your speaking/training career *NOW*, without taking the years required to develop your own competitive System. Become a thoroughly indoctrinated and licensed trainer who can teach the unique Donovan *make more money NOW* System. *Call NOW.*

MAKE MORE MONEY NOW SHOWS

We would like to hear from you how you used this System to *Make More Money NOW* in the real world. So please write to us via email or fax and tell us your success stories. We will invite those with the most dramatic successes to appear on national TV with us to talk about the power of this System.

EDUCATIONAL MATERIALS

Audio cassette album of Alvin's 4 day seminar "Make More Money NOW" with FREE 200 page manual. $99.95.

Video of Alvin's 1 day seminar "Make More Money NOW." $99.95 with FREE 100 page manual.

Vade Mecum organizer. $99.95.

Paper blank PPPL templates. $19.95.

Disk blank PPPL templates. $19.95.

Alvin's 30 minute night time audio tape "Make More Money NOW." $9.95

Client requirement forms on paper. $19.95.

Client requirement forms on disk. $19.95.

Two of Alvin's endless loop tapes, each with a special message to "Make More Money NOW" $19.95.

Meg's daily stress management audio tape. $9.95.